Best Barrett

Jan 79

San Fran

TRADER VIC'S
HELLUVA MAN'S COOKBOOK

BOOKS BY TRADER VIC

TRADER VIC'S HELLUVA MAN'S COOKBOOK
TRADER VIC'S RUM COOKERY AND DRINKERY
TRADER VIC'S BOOK OF MEXICAN COOKING
FRANKLY SPEAKING: TRADER VIC'S OWN STORY
THE MENEHUNES
TRADER VIC'S BARTENDER GUIDE, *Revised*
TRADER VIC'S PACIFIC ISLAND COOKBOOK
TRADER VIC'S BOOK OF FOOD AND DRINK

TRADER VIC'S HELLUVA MAN'S COOKBOOK

BY VICTOR J. BERGERON

ASSISTED BY SHIRLEY SARVIS

ILLUSTRATIONS BY JANE WALWORTH

GARDEN CITY, NEW YORK
DOUBLEDAY & COMPANY, INC.
1976

Library of Congress Cataloging in Publication Data

Bergeron, Victor Jules.
Trader Vic's Helluva man's cookbook.

Includes index.
1. Cookery.   I. Sarvis, Shirley, joint
author.   II. Title.   III. Title: Helluva man's
cookbook.
TX652.B448   641.5
ISBN 0-385-09829-4
Library of Congress Catalog Card Number 75–21210

Copyright © 1976 by Doubleday & Company, Inc.

Printed in the United States of America
9 8 7 6 5 4 3 2

CONTENTS

TRADER VIC'S
HELLUVA MAN'S COOKBOOK

Preface to Things to Come ...

Let's forget about a preface and a dedication and a first and second introduction. Let's go to work and tell you what you ought to know. I've been doing this for a thousand years and I ought to know a little bit about it.

I'd like to start by making a lot of food writers mad, a lot of gourmets thunderstruck, and fifty million Frenchmen driven right out of their cotton pickin' minds by saying that I think French cooking is archaic and a thing of the past. And if you don't think so, just go through France and see all the hamburger and hot dog stands springing up!

Let's start to eat food to stay alive and well and cook the easy way so we can have more time to enjoy ourselves, raise our kids, and see the country—not live to eat and spend most of our time cooking and eating and cleaning up afterward.

Here we are going to do things a little differently. We are going to uncomplicate things. We are going to make things from cans, and the stuff will be fantastic. A lot of you fellows will say that

I'm a silly bastard, but you'll see that you will have fun and at the same time cook fine dishes. Now there are still a lot of wonderful recipes that take time and doing to create, and when they are finished, they are awful damn good to eat. We'll have some of those, too.

But if you're a French cook or a purist on French cooking, don't waste your time with this book. But go ahead and do your French cooking with all the time it takes, and then compare it with my easy way. Here's where we separate the men from the boys. That old crap of spending hours over the stove to make a mediocre meal is ridiculous. I can tell you how to spend just a little time and come up with things that are fabulous.

I'm going to give you an idea here on how to use some fabricated food in your cooking to achieve excellent results. But of course the most fun will be later when you think up your own combinations and have good success. Don't forget that Rome wasn't built in a day, and you don't learn how to cook in three easy lessons. You'll turn out some real beauties before you're good. But when you get the hang of it, you'll be able to turn out a meal in thirty minutes that's fit for a king—and that's no baloney, either. We've got too much going for us in the U.S.A. with good food, good food processors, and good equipment to do it the hard way—especially when the easy way is so damn good and no problem. Not only that, but with simple cooking, you'll be eating healthily and live to be a hundred and ten years old.

And while I am on the subject: you know there is one thing that makes me so damn mad. There is still the guy who likes to buy imported cans of this or that. He is a silly goofball of the first order. We have really good food processors here in the U.S.A. who can foods and freeze them and dehydrate them. And they can start with the greatest natural foods if they will. And the supervision and inspection that the Government gives to our products is the finest in the world. I made a study when I was in France. I went around buying dozens of cans, all the same brand of stuff. And there was no consistency whatsoever in them—no size control, a damn poor pack of stuff right down the line. Now I'm not boosting for canned things or a frozen food line or a dehydrating company. But if you buy imported stuff, you are just not going to get the quality you get in the U.S.A. And our variety is a damn sight better. So don't be so anxious to create status for yourself buying imported. Buy good quality, second-to-none stuff from the U.S.A.

But like in everything else, there are a lot of food processors who are good, some bad, and some just plain lousy. Here's where you come in. Do some tasting and make some judgments. Don't buy one brand of a product and because it's no good condemn all of them. Not long ago, I wanted to find out what canned ravioli sauces were like, and I bought a can of every brand made: Chef Boy-ar-dee meat sauce was the best. Do the same with all the stuff you buy at the beginning. Taste all the brands and you'll be surprised at how quality can vary. And you'll also have the damnedest experience tasting a lot of crappy stuff.

And another thing: The fresh things that we grow here are mostly a whale of a lot better than anything in Europe. You go to Europe and see the cherry trees producing little tiny cherries—just because the Europeans don't prune 'em properly. And the same thing goes for strawberries. A lot of people get fogged into thinking that those little bitty berries are better than ours. Well, they're not. Those are not beautiful fruits; they're just runts. Not long ago, a Sacramento prune farmer told me that the French make all of their own prunes into brandy; they buy California prunes for making their fancy pastries or cooking up something nice.

I get a big kick out of a guy who says he's a gourmet and a great cook. Because, brother, let me tell you a little trade secret: There's no such thing as a gourmet. If you live to be ten thousand, you'll never really know too much about cooking; there's too much to learn. Anybody who calls himself a gourmet is really some kind of a nut. Oh, somebody may know a few dishes and cook them well. But when it comes right down to the nitty gritty, there is just too much food in this world for anyone to know much of anything about it.

Now, fellas, I've seen a lot of purists who follow recipes and I've never seen them work worth a good goddamn so far as cooking goes. If you're going to learn to cook, you've got to learn to think along with it.

Now you're not gonna do this in six easy lessons. It'll take some time. I can tell you how to look for a puddle of juice on top of a hamburger to tell how done it is. But until you do it a time or two for yourself, you won't really know.

But if you think about food as you cook with it and eat it, one thing will lead into the next thing, and you'll be creating and changing recipes. Some of the results will be unbelievably good and a few of them will be unbelievably lousy. What's the fun of cooking if you're just going to follow what some other silly bastard has done?

I've made up recipes here that could actually be cooked in several ways. Maybe doing a particular thing right is really doing it the way the book says or the original authority says. But that doesn't mean that there aren't other ways to do a thing.

What I'm trying to say is that when I'm writing here and I say that this is the way to do it, well, I'm only human. You might think of a helluva lot better way to do it. That's OK.

Believe me, a martini is a martini because it's two thirds gin and one third dry French vermouth, and who the hell drinks it? Nobody! But if you make something that's gin just bruised with vermouth, you've got something that's a lot better than a martini, even if it's not a true martini.

So if you're going to be a purist and stick just to exactly the way the book says and never try anything else, why don't you just go shoot yourself?

When you're cooking, you're cooking not just for the fun of eating, but for enjoyment, for the fun of trying it a different way to see if you can't make it even better. And that's all I'm going to say about it 'cause that covers the whole damn thing.

How to put a menu together is like how long is a piece of string. It can be simple or it can be complicated. The more complicated it is, the tougher it is on you to cook. And believe me, if it's hard on you to prepare, it's going to be doubly hard on your guests to eat it. So give 'em something simple and good.

If you need a fish course and a main course, OK. But that old stuff that says you have to have a lot of courses with soup before and salad and cheese and other stuff after—that's out of date. Forget all those funny little extra things in a menu. Give your guests some nice wholesome food—simple to prepare, easy to eat, and simple to serve, and the people are gonna love you.

Now about wine and booze to go with food: The French have a rigmarole that they go through that you have to have certain wines with certain foods. Most of it's just a big pile of junk, believe me. I'll admit that red wines won't go too well with most fish. But white wine will go with almost anything, even red meats. And if I want an Old Fashioned when I'm eating a meal—or a Whisky Sour—that's what I want. Sometimes I want a Margarita on the Rocks with Mexican food. I don't care. If there's anything I can't stand, it's all those purists who say there's only one way to do a thing. You eat and you drink what you feel like doing, not what somebody tells you.

You may not know this, but you eat with your eyes almost as much as with your mouth. If it doesn't look good, nine times out of ten, it won't taste good. So presentation is very important. So get yourself some nice glassware—within your means. Make up your salads so they look pretty. Have some bright napkins and good-looking silverware. Fix up the dishes that you serve with a touch of parsley, a few slivers of red ginger, a little gob of sour cream. Arranging things thoughtfully is very important for eye appeal. Not only that, it shows care.

Now here I'm talking, but d'you know what? I never remember to do it myself. When I'm cooking at home, to hell with it. But I tell you, in my restaurants we do it.

Now let's start in and cook.

We'll begin at the beginning: You can't make a silk purse out of a sow's ear. Neither can you make good-tasting food out of crappy ingredients. So if you're going to cook something and you want to be proud of it, start out with the best ingredients you can get, handle them as carefully as you can, and you'll have good food.

I don't mean to say that if you're stuck and you just don't have the greatest ingredients you can't make something taste good. You can. I can make anything taste good. But buying poor ingredients to start with is no way to save money. You won't get your satisfaction.

When you really want to do a thing up brown, start with something that's brown already.

Here are a few rules to learn, let's say the basics.

When you're cooking, don't throw in brandy or sherry or rum or wine just to have the pleasure of saying that it's got wine or liquor in it. You've got to do better than that.

Some certain things are good with brandy in them. Some other things are better with rum in them. Some are right with wine in them. Some are better with nothing in them. But think about what you're doing. Don't just go off and put wine and liquors in your cooking for the sake of doing it. Wine and liquor cooking is far overrated, that's a lead-pipe cinch.

I once had a friend who had a lot of dough and a Filipino cook who put brandy or wine in *everything*—salad, soup, main course, dessert, every damn thing. Some of it was good, most of it was lousy.

He thought it was a great joke.

When flaming, sometimes you can make an awful botch out of it. The secret is to have the brandy or rum or whatever liquor you're using warm. Heat the liquor—gently, so you don't evaporate the alcohol—before you light it. As soon as the flame shows, begin spooning the liquid up to let air get to it. But don't dilute the liquor with other ingredients until the flaming is over, because dilution will cut down on your fire.

A lot of people like to brown things in the same deep pot as they're going to stew in. I'm not for that. I don't like a deep casserole or stewpot for browning. I'll use a big frying pan for browning, a big cast-iron frying pan—not Teflon. Then you can brown and see what you're doing, and later transfer the browned meat to the stewpot.

When you're through and want to get the juices out, just put in a little broth or water and swish it around and scrape it out. It's a lot better to brown separately and put it in your stewpot after browning.

And you know what? A lot of those dishes that call for stewing in a casserole or stewpot can cook right in the frying pan. You don't even need a deep pot. Hell, there's nothing better than cooking in a cast-iron frying pan with a good cover.

When you are thickening a sauce or a gravy, you can tell how thick it's ever going to get and how thick it is going to stay by bringing it to a slow rolling boil. At that boiling point, it's as thick as it's ever going to get—unless you cook it so long that it reduces down.

A little vanilla does for cakes what Tabasco does for savory things—points the flavors up and rounds them out. If you use a lot of it, you wind up tasting vanilla (or Tabasco); use a little and everything tastes good.

If you fry something lightly and then want to keep it warm, put it into a 350° oven and *keep the door open.* In other words, just keep the nicely fried food at its temperature. Don't increase it or you'll louse it up. But don't fry anything for a long time. It will get tough as hell if you do. And then it won't make any difference where or how you keep it warm.

Now there is sour and there is sweet. And there *is* a place for both at the same time. So don't make a thing be only sour when it should have a little sugar to make it taste good. A good example is stewed tomatoes. Just a touch of sugar counters their sourness and makes all the difference in the world. The same goes for salad dressing and tomato sauce. Now don't be a damn fool and go overboard. All you need is a touch on the end of a spoon. *Don't use too much.*

Salt and pepper. How much do you . . . ? No way. Use it to suit your taste. So start out easy and don't use as much as you think you should and most likely you'll be right.

Now we come to fat, grease, oil, butter—anything that is fat. Nothing tastes good—cakes, cookies, candy, vegetables, meat, etc., etc., etc.—without a little fat of some kind. Now the trick is how much you use: lots and louse everything up, or so little that it doesn't count. This, fellows, is another place where you separate the men from the boys. And you won't learn the answer in six easy lessons.

The best way is to start your cooking project using as little fat as you can, and then add a little bit more and build to where your result is pleasing.

Most recipes call for too much fat, and then the wrong kinds— for instance *olive oil*. I don't keep it in the house. Boy, can I hear groans from the experts. Let them groan; they're archaic. When I want a salad oil, I use safflower or peanut oil.

The important thing in choosing which fat to use is to use the appropriate fat with the appropriate thing. For example, when frying meat, use the fat from the meat you are frying: render out a piece of beef fat, then fry your beefsteak in that. Rub a piece of lamb fat around your frying pan before you do your lamb chops. Pork has enough fat so you don't need more. Use bacon fat when you need that flavor. Use butter where you need that rich taste. Think.

Now let's talk about meat, beef first.

If you go to a shop and buy a steak and get a tough piece of meat, nine times out of ten it's your own fault. You probably went to a shop that wasn't a quality butcher shop.

But buy at a good shop which handles quality meat, and you'll usually get a quality piece of meat.

Now I don't know of anyone who can look inside of a steer after it's killed and skinned and tell that he's going to get tender meat. Neither can your butcher tell you this a hundred per cent of the time. So if your good butcher usually gives you good meat and today the steak is tough, give the poor bastard a break. Don't chew the poor guy out because you get an occasional bum steer. I've been doing business with the same meat packers for thirty years, and, on and off, this disappointment happens to me, too. . . . Well, then, of course if you keep on getting tough steak, change your butcher.

In the next chapter, with the help of some color photos, I'm going to try and explain what to look for in steaks and roasts.

Now remember this. I'm doing what *I* believe and it's not the *only* way. But I'm trying to give you a guide. So, use your own bean and figure things out so they're right for you.

First Things First: COOKING MEAT

Now let's start with a simple explanation about cooking meat. Hold your hand, palm up, perfectly relaxed. Now feel the fleshy part of your thumb; it's soft and all you feel is soft tissue. Now, tense the muscles of your thumb; and now the soft part has changed to a certain firmness. This same thing takes place in steak tissue when you cook it. The tissue gradually tenses and tightens up in proportion to the amount and length of heat that it gets—until the meat is like a piece of leather. The same thing will happen to chicken, pork, roasts, pot roasts, etc., etc., etc. Once you've cooked the meat too hard, too well done, possibly burnt, the only way you can make it tender again is to cook it for several hours with liquid until the tissue finally gives up and goes limp again.

COOKING A STEAK

Holy Toledo, there are more ways to do this than Heinz has beans in all his cans. But let's do it my way and if you don't like it . . .

The fire for cooking steaks is of utmost importance. It has to be hot. Now don't put your steak in anything but a *hot* frying pan or onto anything but a *hot* barbecue grill. If you do, you'll boil your steak in its own juice, and all the juices will run out the bottom, and when you turn it over, it will look like hell and be as dry as an old shoe. There's just no use monkeying around with a low fire. Use a hot fire and get it over with.

Two reasons why a *hot* fire is so important:

1. Ever since man used fire, he has liked the flavor of burnt meat; and a well-browned piece of meat *is* burnt meat, and that gives you your flavor. Now don't burn the hell out of your steak or you will be eating charcoal.

2. What happens when you heat a piece of meat is that the juices want to get away from the heat. So to prevent that, you have to sear the steak on both sides and even around the edges of a thick steak—so that the searing will keep the juices inside. You can't sear the meat with a cold fire. Just to illustrate this in another way, let me tell you how the Chinese sometimes cook a duck. They clean a duck all out on the inside. Then they tie the neck with a piece of string and fill the cavity with spiced soup and tie up the other end the same way. After that, they cover the outside skin with a soy sauce and honey mixture, and hang the duck in the air to dry. Then they put the thing into a barbecue pit. The process then works almost like a pressure cooker. As the soup heats, it builds up pressure and boils and at the same time cooks the duck meat tender. The soup inside of the duck is like the juices inside a steak; as these liquids heat, they bubble and try to escape. The dry soy-honey glaze on the skin of the duck keeps the soup inside the duck; the brown searing on a steak keeps the juices inside the steak.

If you're cooking a steak in a frying pan, put a piece of steak fat on the pan, and if it starts to sizzle right off the bat, the pan is hot. You can tell yourself if your barbecue or broiling grill is hot.

So learn to cook steak by the touch system: Cook it over a hot fire good and brown on one side, then turn it over and start on the other side. Wait a few moments, and poke the steak in the center with your finger. If it's still very soft, it's too raw. Leave the steak and, shortly, poke it again. Before long, you will feel it start to stiffen, and that is medium rare. After that, changes happen quickly, and in a matter of moments, the steak goes from medium rare to medium to well done. Now don't try to poke the steak and judge it the instant that you turn it over. Because right at that point, the heat has driven the juices down in the meat away from the browned side of the meat; they are no longer up against the cooked part of the steak because they have been trying to get away from that hot-fire side of the steak. The meat will feel hard if you poke it right then, and it won't be an accurate test. Wait just a half minute, and the juices will have rushed back toward the top of the steak away from the heat. Then you can make an accurate judgment.

Now you are not going to learn this whole technique in this easy lesson. I didn't; no one does. Trial and error is the thing. But after a while, you will be able to cook fifty or a hundred steaks, and every damn one of 'em will turn out the way you want them because you will know how they should feel; it's that simple.

A friend of mine now long gone, Sam Morse of Carmel, was the damnedest barbecuer. He had a big pair of tongs—hell, they were fourteen inches long and made out of heavy iron—which he used for turning the steaks over. Well, Sam would put the steaks on the grill and brown a side, and then turn them. Then he'd start to bounce the tongs on the steak. And he could tell by the way they bounced how done the steaks were. And, believe me, he never missed—rare, medium rare, medium. Nobody ever ate a well-done steak at Sam's barbecue; that was considered a sacrilege.

Now more specifically:

For a fairly thin steak, about three-fourths inch thick: Brown it well over a hot fire on one side. Turn. Within a half minute, put your finger on it to test it, and then leave the steak on the fire until it's done the way you like it.

If the steak is over one inch thick, you may have to turn it a couple of times.

When steaks are two to three inches thick, start out with five minutes on a side and you might even sear the edges (not the fat edge, but where the steak was cut). Then feel your steak. If it's too soft in the middle, you may have to turn it over several times. But keep feeling the center.

In cooking a very thin steak, maybe one-fourth inch thick, as for a steak sandwich: Put the steak into a hot, hot greased pan or griddle. Count to five. Turn. Salt and pepper. Count to five again, and take it off the fire. Just as soon as juices begin to show on top, it's done.

And that is another indication of steak doneness: After you've first turned the steak, little puddles of juice on the top mean medium rare to medium, and big puddles of juice mean well done. This test works even if you're cooking a thick hamburger: Brown it fast and well on one side. Turn it over. When juices show in the cracks on the brown side, the meat is medium rare.

MORE ON HOW TO COOK A HAMBURGER

Most people just cook a hamburger to bits. I think some restaurants cook a lousy hamburger. More guys don't know how to cook a hamburger because they boil it.

In doing a thin hamburger: Put it onto a hot greased griddle or pan. As soon as a puddle of juice shows on the top, turn it, count to ten, and pop it in the bun (the second side won't be too brown, but you'll have the good brown color on the side that shows *and* juiciness).

If it's a thick hamburger: Make the patty, bang it on a hot greased griddle or pan. Cook for a bit until it browns well on one side, turn it over. When the juice starts to show through in the cracks on the browned side, it's cooked to medium rare. Get it the hell off the fire *now!*

Now when I say hot, the damn thing has got to be smoking hot. Some people's idea of a hot griddle won't even make spit sizzle!

Japanese Hamburger

If you want to do a Japanese hamburger, very, very nice . . .

You just dash a generous amount of Japanese sake (rice wine) into your hamburger meat before you shape it and fry it, and see what it does. You'll be surprised! You don't need any other spices except salt and pepper.

Chinese Hamburgers

2 pounds ground chuck
About 1 teaspoon salt
About 1 teaspoon freshly
  ground black pepper
4 dashes Tabasco
3 tablespoons Kikkoman soy
  sauce

1 cup finely chopped water
  chestnuts
¼ cup minced green onions
  with part of green tops

Lightly but thoroughly mix all ingredients. Shape into 4 large patties. Broil over charcoal or in oven broiler, or grill or panbroil to doneness you desire. Makes 4 servings.

Lamb Salisbury

Well, these are just plain hamburgers made from lamb instead of beef and with a little difference. I like them better than beef.

Use *only* the lean part of lamb, no fat. If you include the fat, the lamb will taste too strong. Have the lamb ground for you as for hamburger.

2 pounds lean lamb, ground
About ½ teaspoon salt
½ teaspoon ground nutmeg
About ¼ teaspoon freshly
  ground black pepper

1 cup peeled, seeded, and diced
  fresh tomato
½ cup fine soft bread crumbs
Cucumber sauce (recipe below)

Lightly but thoroughly mix all ingredients. Form into 6 patties, each about 1 inch thick. Broil on both sides—over charcoal or in oven broiler or in a heavy frying pan with a little oil to prevent sticking—until done to your liking. Serve with cucumber sauce spooned over. Makes 3 or 6 servings.

Cucumber sauce   In a heavy frying pan, sauté ⅔ cup peeled, seeded, and finely diced fresh cucumber in 3 tablespoons butter until tender-crisp. Stir in 1 teaspoon paprika. Remove from heat and gradually stir in ⅔ cup commercial sour cream. Return to low heat and just heat through. Correct seasoning with salt and pepper.

Crêpinettes

My mother grew up in the Pyrenees, a little town called La Barthe-de-Neste. A couple of times a year, her family, along with some neighbors, would kill a pig. And they would make smoked ham, sausages, and a variety of other meats. One thing they made were *crêpinettes*. Really they're fresh pork patties. They are damn good. To do them right, you have to wrap them in caul fat, the membrane around a pig's tummy that looks like lace. It's hard to get caul. You usually have to order it ahead from a good butcher shop. Or sometimes you can find it at a pork butcher shop in Chinatown. Once you get the caul, keep it soaking in cold water until you use it, so that it doesn't dry out. If you can't get the caul, you can do without: just brown the patties the same way, slowly, in a small amount of butter and finish in the oven.

The spicing here is only a suggestion. You can vary it to suit yourself. (As you are blending the spices, fry a small amount of the mixture, taste, and correct seasoning.)

You can also serve these with a paprika sauce or country gravy.

2 pounds lean boneless pork (shoulder, butt, loin ends)
4 slices farm-style white bread, crusts removed
1 cup heavy (whipping) cream
1 cup half and half (half milk and half cream)
2 tablespoons brandy
1 egg, beaten
3 tablespoons finely minced green onions (white part only)
1½ teaspoons salt
1¼ teaspoons freshly ground white pepper

½ teaspoon each ground nutmeg and ginger and crumbled dried sage
⅜ teaspoon each crumbled dried thyme and bay leaf
¼ teaspoon freshly ground black pepper
⅛ teaspoon ground mace
1/16 teaspoon ground cloves
6 sprigs fresh parsley
Caul fat (presoaked)
About 1 cup fine soft bread crumbs
Butter

Put pork through grinder fit with finest blade twice. Soak bread in cream and half and half. Mix very thoroughly with wooden spoon or clean hands the pork, soaked bread with liquid, brandy, egg, onions, salt, spices, and herbs. Dipping hands into cold water, shape mixture into 6 patties, each about 4 inches in diameter and 1½ inches deep. Place a sprig of parsley in center of each. Wrap to enclose with a piece of caul cut just the size to cover patty (do not overlap caul ends). Roll in bread crumbs to coat. In a heavy frying pan over low and medium heat brown patties well on both sides in a small amount of butter, about 30 minutes total. Then transfer to a 350° oven and bake for 20 minutes. Spoon any loose crisp crumbs over top. Makes 6 servings.

Indonesian Lamb Roast

2- to 3-pound lamb rib roast (single rack of lamb)
Javanese saté marinade (recipe below) or Trader Vic's Shish
   Kebob Meat Marinade prepared according to package directions
Peanut sauce (below)

Trim lamb of all fat, completely to the rib bones. Coat lamb with marinade, cover, and marinate for 12 to 24 hours. Drain off marinade. Wrap bone ends in foil to prevent burning. Place on rack in open roasting pan, rib side down. Bake in a 375° oven until meat thermometer reads 140° (or 170° if you prefer lamb well done), about 20 minutes. Carve between ribs. Pass peanut sauce to ladle over. Makes 2 to 4 servings.

Javanese saté marinade   Mix together thoroughly ⅓ cup fresh lemon juice, 2 teaspoons honey, 2 teaspoons Trader Vic's Javanese Saté Spice, ½ teaspoon salt, ¼ teaspoon freshly ground black pepper, 1 onion, finely chopped, and 1 clove garlic, minced or mashed.

Peanut sauce   Sauté 1 tablespoon minced green onions with part of green tops in 1 tablespoon butter until limp. Stir in ⅔ cup chicken broth, ¼ cup dry white table wine, 2 tablespoons chunk-style peanut butter, 1 teaspoon Trader Vic's Javanese Saté Spice, and 1 teaspoon Kikkoman soy sauce. Cook and stir to blend well. Gradually add ⅓ cup heavy (whipping) cream. Cook and stir over high heat until liquid reduces to thin sauce consistency.

Malagasy Pepper Steak

Go to a good deli or specialty food store and get some little canned green peppercorns. Mainly, they come from Madagascar, Malagasy Republic. These peppercorns are tremendously flavorful little things, absolutely scrumptious. They are not like the hard black peppercorns; these are soft, pliable, and mushy. I use them to make a Pepper Steak that tastes awfully good and puts a regular steak to shame.

You can store this Malagasy butter in your freezer if you want, and then when you're ready to make a steak, cut off a chunk and let it thaw and use it. You can also use this butter on other things, such as fillet of sole or chicken.

Choose your favorite cut of broiling steak, and broil it to one stage less done than you want it when finished. In other words, broil your steak as usual, but if you like it rare, cook it to very rare; if you like it medium-rare, cook it rare; if you want it medium, cook it medium-rare. Then put about 4 tablespoons of Malagasy pepper butter (recipe below) on top, and run the steak under the broiler until the butter melts and glazes to golden brown.

Malagasy pepper butter   Combine in a mixing bowl 1 cup soft butter, 1 egg yolk, 2 generous tablespoons drained green peppercorns (*poivre vert*), 4 teaspoons minced green onions with part of green tops, 1 tablespoon minced fresh parsley, ¼ teaspoon crumbled dried tarragon, 1 teaspoon fresh lemon juice, 1 teaspoon brandy, ½ teaspoon Worcestershire sauce, ½ teaspoon Dijon-style mustard, and a dash of Tabasco.

Hans's Beef Tartare

Our head captain in our San Francisco restaurant is Hans Brandt. He is a perfectionist from the word go. He makes the damnedest beef tartare in the city.

This is Hans's refinement on everyone else's beef tartare. Over the years, watching and caring at Trader Vic's, he has observed what people like best in their beef tartare. And over many earlier years of working all over Europe, he picked up best tips from best headwaiters about the making of this North European specialty.

(Hans says that beef tartare originated in the eastern countries of Europe, in the cold northern countries where people needed a lot of protein in order to fight against the elements. The horsemen and/or cowboys put raw beef under their saddles. As they rode, the beef became tenderized. Once at their destination where there was no fuel for cooking, they could spice the beef and eat it raw.

Through years of civilization, the formula for beef tartare has likewise become more civilized, more refined. Still, it is a specialty in northern countries as Germany and Denmark—never in the southern places.)

Some makers of beef tartare mix all of the seasoning ingredients together first, then mix them with the beef. Hans does not agree with that procedure. He thinks that it is essential to do all of the mixing at once in order to keep texture fascination, as well as to provide the best taste.

Serve with toasted thin slices of rye bread, unbuttered.

Place a round dinner serving plate in freezer to chill well. Present in the center of a large silver pedestal platter:

6 ounces beef fillet or fillet tips completely trimmed of fat, once ground (Shape in a mound. Score lightly with two dinner knives to give beef the appearance of having been chopped, not ground.)

Surround on tray with a glass cup of each:

Dehydrated minced onions, soaked in water until reconstituted and drained (or finely minced fresh onions)
Anchovy fillets, minced as finely as possible
1 raw egg yolk, all chalaza removed
Finely chopped fresh parsley
Drained capers

On serving cart place:
Cut fresh lemons
Small glass cruet of safflower oil
Brandy
Worcestershire sauce
Black pepper grinder
Monosodium glutamate
Salt
Limestone lettuce leaves and/or watercress sprigs

Lift meat into a shallow wooden salad bowl. Squeeze on juice of about one half lemon. Sprinkle with about 2 teaspoons oil.

Sprinkle with about 2 teaspoons brandy. Sprinkle liberally with Worcestershire sauce (about ¾ teaspoon). Grind on plenty of black pepper to season. Sprinkle with about 4 teaspoons onions. Sprinkle with about 1 teaspoon anchovies (not too much or it will taste salty and fishy). Add egg yolk. Sprinkle with about 2 teaspoons parsley. Sprinkle with about 4 teaspoons capers. Sprinkle with about ⅛ teaspoon monosodium glutamate. Sprinkle with salt to season, about ⅛ teaspoon. Using two large serving spoons or tablespoons, lightly but thoroughly mix all ingredients together using a chopping action. Lift mixture into center of the chilled serving plate. Using two dinner knives, shape mixture into a square about 4 inches each side. Using the knives and a light chopping motion, score mixture over the top about every ⅛ inch, vertically, horizontally, and diagonally. Present it so that it looks chopped, and lifted. Garnish with lettuce and/or watercress, leaving plenty of the white plate showing. Serve. Provide salt, pepper grinder, additional cut lemons, and Worcestershire for eater to add according to taste. Makes 1 serving.

Sweetbreads Trader Vic Style

When I was growing up, for our Sunday dinners, we'd have sweetbreads a great many times. So sweetbreads were one of the first things I learned to cook—along with bread pudding, frog's legs, and a million kinds of soup. I'm still wild about sweetbreads. And I still say that this way is the best way to cook sweetbreads.

Now you can serve these just the way they are. Or if you want to be real fancy, serve them on two or three *thin* slices of butter-frizzled Canadian bacon.

Prepared sweetbreads (recipe below)
Flour
3 to 4 tablespoons butter
½ cup finely chopped shallots
1 small can (2 ounces) button mushrooms, drained and cut in half

½ cup dry white table wine
2 tablespoons chicken broth
1 teaspoon Worcestershire sauce
Salt and freshly ground black pepper
Finely chopped fresh parsley

Prepared sweetbreads Soak 1 pound veal sweetbreads in several changes of cold water for 2 hours. Then soak for 1 hour longer in 1 quart cold water and 1 tablespoon vinegar. Gently pull off as much of the outside membrane as possible without tearing the sweetbreads. Trim off all tubes and any discolored portions. Put sweetbreads in a saucepan with 1 quart cold water, 1 teaspoon salt, and 1 teaspoon fresh lemon juice. Heat to simmering, then slowly simmer, uncovered, for 15 minutes. Drain, plunge into ice water, and let stand for 5 minutes. Drain. Dry on paper towels.

Cut sweetbreads into about ¾-inch pieces. Lightly flour them. In a large heavy frying pan over medium-high heat, brown sweetbreads in butter. Add shallots and toss. Add mushrooms, wine, chicken broth, and Worcestershire. Cook, gently turning, until the liquid reduces to a thin cloaking sauce. Season generously with salt and pepper. Sprinkle very lightly with parsley. Makes 2 to 3 servings.

Tongue Vinaigrette

You can do this same thing with chilled sliced tongue and room-temperature vinaigrette.

3½-pound corned beef tongue	1 bay leaf
Water	¼ teaspoon whole black
1 peeled onion studded with 4	peppercorns
whole cloves	Vinaigrette sauce (recipe below)
1 stalk celery with leaves	

Put tongue into a kettle with cold water to cover, heat to boiling, and simmer for 5 minutes. Pour off water. Cover tongue again with cold water, add onion, celery, bay leaf, and peppercorns. Cover, heat to boiling, then simmer until tongue is tender, about 3 hours. While hot, remove skin from tongue and trim off excess root tissue. Return tongue to broth to keep warm until serving time, or to cool. Prepare vinaigrette sauce (below). If you wish, slowly heat vinaigrette just to warm through. Slice tongue, and pass vinaigrette to ladle over. Makes 6 to 8 servings.

Vinaigrette sauce Beat together well with a fork 1 cup salad oil, ½ cup mild white wine vinegar, 1 teaspoon dry mustard, about ½ teaspoon salt, about ¼ teaspoon freshly ground black pepper,

4 tablespoons minced green bell peppers, 4 tablespoons snipped chives (or 1 tablespoon minced green onions with part of green tops), 1 tablespoon minced fresh parsley, 1 teaspoon minced capers, and 2 hard-cooked eggs, finely chopped. Taste and correct seasoning with salt and pepper. Makes about 2 cups.

Regal Beef in Red Wine

In order to do this really fast, make the wine sauce ahead of time. Then near serving time, reheat it, quickly sauté the beef, put the beef and the sauce together, and serve.

You *have* to sauté the beef *very* fast over a *hot* fire—to brown the meat on the outside and keep it rare on the inside. If you sauté in unclarified butter, it will smoke and brown; that is OK.

1 tablespoon minced shallots	**Freshly ground black pepper**
3½ tablespoons soft butter	**4 tablespoons flour**
1⅓ cups dry red table wine	**1½ pounds top sirloin or fillet**
1 can (10½ ounces) beef	**tip (or other tender, lean**
bouillon (undiluted)	**beef), cut into ¾-inch cubes**
1 small bay leaf	**4 tablespoons butter**
¼ teaspoon crumbled dried	**Finely chopped fresh parsley**
thyme	
1 large clove garlic, minced or	
mashed	

In a wide frying pan, sauté shallots in 1½ tablespoons of the soft butter just until heated and coated with drippings. Add wine, bouillon, bay leaf, thyme, garlic, and a generous grinding of black pepper. Cook over high heat, stirring, until liquid is reduced to 2 cups. Mix remaining 2 tablespoons soft butter with 2 tablespoons of the flour to make a paste. Remove the wine mixture from heat, and quickly whisk in flour mixture. Return to heat, and boil for 30 seconds. Remove bay leaf. Keep sauce hot. Put remaining 2 table-spoons flour in a clean paper or plastic bag. Add beef and shake to coat. In a large, heavy frying pan over high heat, quickly brown beef in the 4 tablespoons butter until cubes are well browned on the outside and rare on the inside. Fold into hot wine sauce, sprin-kle lightly with parsley, and serve immediately. Makes 4 servings.

Quick Stroganoff and Quick Stroganoff Supper Sandwich

Buy ground veal—medium grind. Put a *lot* of butter into a very hot frying pan. Add veal and turn and fry and brown quickly, separating it so it will granulate. Lower heat. Stir in plenty of salt and pepper, enough commercial sour cream to moisten it up well, and a generous shot of Worcestershire. Serve it that way. Garnish with watercress.

Or put it on a buttered, toasted English muffin or toasted bun or buttered toast for an open sandwich.

Now don't use too much sour cream or it'll get leaky.

Julienne Veal in Sour Cream Sauce

1½ pounds veal for scaloppine (boneless veal cutlet pounded very thinly)
2 tablespoons flour
Salt and freshly ground black pepper
About 5 tablespoons butter
4 tablespoons minced green onions (white part only)
2 teaspoons paprika

½ cup dry white table wine
1½ cups commercial sour cream
1 tablespoon Worcestershire sauce
¼ cup finely chopped toasted filberts (hazelnuts)
2 teaspoons finely chopped fresh parsley

Slice veal into strips about 3 inches by ¼ inch. Combine flour, ¾ teaspoon salt, and ½ teaspoon pepper in a clean paper bag. Add veal, and shake to coat. In large heavy frying pan, sauté veal in 4 tablespoons of the butter over high heat just until tender and lightly browned. (Butter will brown.) Remove from pan and keep warm. Melt remaining butter in the frying pan, add onions, and sauté until limp. Stir in paprika. Add wine and cook and stir to loosen and blend drippings and until liquid reduces to about 2 tablespoons. Reduce heat to low. Stir in sour cream and Worcestershire. Season generously with additional salt. Fold veal into sour cream, heat through, sprinkle with filberts and parsley, and serve. Makes 4 generous servings.

Pork Mozzarella

This is also good with lettuce and a little mayonnaise in a broiled English muffin sandwich—with beer.

8 thin slices boneless pork loin
  or cutlet (about ¾ pound
  total)
4 tablespoons finely peeled,
  seeded, and diced fresh tomato
4 slices mozzarella cheese
  (about 6 ounces total)

Salt and freshly ground black
  pepper
Flour
Equal parts salad oil and butter

Place pork between sheets of waxed paper and pound very thin. For each serving: Place 1 tablespoon tomato and a slice of cheese on 1 piece of pork; top with a second slice of pork, pressing edges together well. Season both sides well with salt and pepper. Dust with flour and shake off excess. Repeat to make 4 servings. In a heavy frying pan over medium heat, lightly brown meat on both sides in a small amount of oil and butter. Then bake in 350° oven for 6 minutes, until cheese melts. Makes 4 servings.

Bourbon Meat Balls in Sour Cream Sauce

1 pound ground chuck
½ pound ground veal
4 tablespoons grated fresh
  onions
Finely chopped fresh parsley
Salt and freshly ground black
  pepper
½ teaspoon ground allspice

½ teaspoon ground nutmeg
½ cup fine soft bread crumbs
1 egg, lightly beaten
2 cups commercial sour cream
1 tablespoon butter
3 tablespoons bourbon
4 teaspoons Worcestershire
  sauce

Mix together lightly but thoroughly the chuck, veal, 2 tablespoons of the onions, 2 tablespoons parsley, 1½ teaspoons salt, ½ teaspoon pepper, the allspice, nutmeg, bread crumbs, egg, and 3 tablespoons of the sour cream. Shape into small balls no larger than 1 inch in diameter. Place well apart in a buttered shallow baking pan. Bake in a 500° oven for about 6 minutes, just until browned and barely done; stir once. Pour off excess drippings. Loosen crisp brown drippings. In a large frying pan, sauté remaining 2 tablespoons onions in the butter until golden and tender. Reduce heat to low. Add bourbon, and cook and stir until liquid almost disappears. Stir in remaining sour cream, the Worcestershire, and loosened brown drippings from meat balls; and just heat through. Season sauce generously with salt and pepper. Fold in meat balls, and just heat through. Sprinkle with parsley. Makes 5 to 6 servings.

Meat Balls and Hamburger Dumplings

My Aunt Rose cooked these dumplings for me every time she wanted to give me a treat. Ground meat in the dumpling dough made the dumplings taste good and look good. These are not ordinary dumplings.

Quick tomato sauce (recipe below)	**Salt and freshly ground black pepper**
Meat balls (recipe below)	**Chopped fresh parsley**
Dumplings (recipe below)	

Prepare tomato sauce and heat to bubbling. Prepare meat balls, add to sauce, and return sauce to gently bubbling. Prepare dumplings and drop by heaping spoonfuls (making 8 dumplings) onto gently bubbling liquid. Cover kettle tightly, and cook for 40 minutes (do not lift cover; keep liquid gently bubbling). Lift dumplings from liquid, and arrange as a border around a warm, deep serving platter. Taste sauce and correct seasoning with salt and pepper. Turn meat balls in sauce into center of platter. Sprinkle lightly with parsley. Makes 4 servings.

Quick tomato sauce In a large kettle, sauté 1 medium-sized onion, finely chopped; 1 cup chopped celery; and 1 carrot, peeled and finely chopped; in 3 tablespoons butter until limp. Stir in 1 large can (1 pound 12 ounces) peeled whole tomatoes (preferably Italian pear-shaped tomatoes), broken up; ¼ cup dry white table wine; 1 tablespoon minced fresh parsley; 2 cloves garlic, minced or mashed; ¼ teaspoon sugar; ½ teaspoon salt; ¼ teaspoon pepper; and a dash of Tabasco.

Meat balls   Mix together lightly but thoroughly 1½ pounds ground chuck, 2 tablespoons minced fresh parsley, 2 tablespoons grated fresh onions, 1½ teaspoons salt, ½ teaspoon freshly ground black pepper, ½ cup fine soft bread crumbs, 1 beaten egg, 2 tablespoons dry white or red table wine, and 1 teaspoon A.1. sauce. Shape into small walnut-sized balls. In a heavy frying pan, brown quickly on all sides in a small amount of salad oil.

Dumplings   Fry about 2 ounces ground chuck in a heavy frying pan until lightly browned and crumbly. Season well with salt, pepper, and crumbled dried oregano. Cool. Make one half recipe of My Dumplings (page 113), adding this browned meat.

APPETIZERS
TO KILL YOUR APPETITE

I wonder where the heck the guy who calls these appetizers ever got that idea. They kill my appetite every time I eat them.

Hamburger Appetizers

You know what you can do that's easy.

Take hamburger (ground round)—raw—and flavor it up with salt and pepper. Shape it into little balls no bigger than 1 inch in diameter, roll them in grated Parmesan cheese, and then fry them in butter (medium heat). But fry just enough so the cheese gets stuck all over; the meat'll be almost raw in the middle. It'll taste fancy. Serve each one on a stick.

Potted Shrimp

Potted shrimp is an old English recipe. Very good. Be sure your shrimp aren't stinky. Great dish.

Heat 6 tablespoons unsalted butter over medium-high heat in a frying pan until it bubbles. Add ⅓ pound tiny shrimp, ¾ teaspoon ground mace, and ⅛ teaspoon freshly ground black pepper. Sauté until shrimp are heated through. Put into a pot and press down. Heat about 3 tablespoons more unsalted butter until it bubbles; pour enough of this bubbling butter over shrimp to seal them generously. Cover and keep in refrigerator. Allow to return to room temperature before serving. Spread on crisp Armenian sesame cracker bread or crisp thin water wafers.

Hinky Dinks

My first restaurant was Hinky Dinks before it was Trader Vic's. I used to do some cooking there, and I made these damn things, and the people liked 'em.

Buy some miniature cream puffs—about 2 inches in diameter—from a good bakery. Or maybe you can get your old lady to bake some for you. Cut each in two, with about ⅔ of the puff for the bottom and ⅓ for the top. Fill with a good chicken salad, and top with a generous sprinkling of fresh pepper cress or little sprigs of watercress. Close lightly.

Jeanne's Quick Chile con Queso

My daughter Jeanne is a great homemaker and cook. For Christmas, she always makes me a steamed carrot pudding and a plum pudding and two or three other little goodies, cakes, and cookies. And she makes a damn good *chile con queso*.

Now remember that after you melt the cheese down this thing is gonna be pretty hot. So don't put your little cookie in there and eat it right down or it'll burn your little tum to beat the band. Let it cool a little before you dip in your corn chip.

Add some freshly ground black pepper if you like it. Serve with crisp corn chips for dipping.

1 pound Velveeta cheese
(pasteurized process cheese
spread)
1 can (7 ounces) Ortega green
chile sauce
1 can or jar (2 ounces)
pimentos, drained and
chopped

1 clove garlic, minced or
mashed
¼ cup heavy (whipping) cream

Heat and stir all ingredients together in a chafing dish set over a low flame or in the top part of a double boiler over boiling water. Serve warm, not hot. Makes about 2 cups.

ABOUT DIPS

I'm hot for dips at parties. They save a lot of work and time, and your guests invariably like them. They are easy, good, not too filling, and you can express yourself a thousand ways with them.

Here are a few. Think up some of your own.

I don't like just plain cream cheese. It's too sticky.

There are some potato chips that are not potato chips. They're called potato chips, but they're made out of dehydrated mashed potatoes. You can read that on the package. Get those little babies for your dips, because they're the best-tasting things you've ever wrapped your lips around. They're better than real potato chips.

Dill Dip

Dip with potato chips.

1 cup commercial sour cream
⅓ cup mayonnaise
4 teaspoons dried dill weed
2 teaspoons beau monde
seasoning
Generous dash of Tabasco

3 tablespoons minced fresh
parsley
2 tablespoons minced green
onions with part of green tops
¼ teaspoon fresh lemon juice

Stir all ingredients together. Makes about 1½ cups.

Clam Dip

This and the following two dips are no different from a thousand other dips. Except that I've added some ginger. Now go down to a Chinese store and buy yourself a jar of Chinese sweet red ginger. Wash it off, chop it up, and stick it into these dips.

This is good with the olives and without the ginger. But it's fantastic with the ginger and without the olives.

Serve with potato chips.

1 large package (8 ounces) cream cheese, softened
2 tablespoons mayonnaise
About 1½ teaspoons A.1. sauce
About ⅛ teaspoon salt
Generous grinding of black pepper
1 tablespoon minced green onions with part of green tops

1 can (6½ ounces) minced clams, drained
1 tablespoon chopped black olives or about 1½ teaspoons rinsed, drained, and minced Chinese sweet red ginger

Beat cheese until light and fluffy. Thoroughly stir in remaining ingredients. Makes about 2 cups.

Crab Dip

If you're doing this without the ginger, use the celery for the crunch. If you're adding the ginger, use water chestnuts instead of celery.

Dip this up with thin crisp wheat wafers or potato chips.

¾ cup commercial sour cream
1½ tablespoons mayonnaise
1 tablespoon minced green onions with part of green tops
About ¼ teaspoon Worcestershire sauce
¼ pound (1 cup) flaked crab meat

¼ pound finely diced celery or water chestnuts
Salt and freshly ground black pepper to season
½ to 1 teaspoon rinsed, drained, and minced Chinese sweet red ginger (optional)

Thoroughly mix sour cream, mayonnaise, onions, and Worcestershire. Stir in remaining ingredients. Makes about 2 cups.

Tuna Dip

Dip this with potato chips.

1 cup commercial sour cream
⅓ cup mayonnaise
1 teaspoon fresh lemon juice
Generous dash of Tabasco
1 can (3½ ounces) solid white
 tuna, flaked (do not drain)
3 tablespoons finely chopped
 fresh parsley

2 tablespoons minced green
 onions with part of green tops
About 2 teaspoons rinsed,
 drained, and minced Chinese
 sweet red ginger (optional)
Salt and freshly ground black
 pepper

Stir together thoroughly sour cream, mayonnaise, lemon juice, and Tabasco. Stir in tuna with oil, parsley, onions, ginger, and a generous amount of salt and pepper to season. Makes about 2 cups.

Pine Nut Cheese Balls

Once in a while, I write one cookbook after another. Sometimes a recipe is so good that I take it out of one book and put it into another. These Pine Nut Cheese Balls are in my Mexican book. They're good, so I'm putting 'em in here. You may not have the Mexican book.

2 large packages (8 ounces
 each) cream cheese, softened
About 3 tablespoons heavy
 (whipping) cream
¾ teaspoon salt
3 tablespoons finely chopped
 green bell pepper

2 tablespoons minced green
 onions with part of green tops
2 tablespoons finely chopped
 drained canned pimentos
Very lightly toasted pine nuts

With a fork, mash cheese and blend with enough cream to moisten. Stir until smooth. Stir in salt, green pepper, onions, and pimentos. Chill if necessary in order to handle. Shape into small balls no larger than 1 inch in diameter. Roll in pine nuts to coat. Makes about 3 dozen cheese balls.

Trader Vic's Quick Appetizer Spread

You spread this onto crisp crackers (saltines or wheat) for an appetizer. If you want to change it into a dip for potato chips or crackers, gradually stir in enough salad oil to make it of dipping consistency. If you want to vary it, add chopped hard-cooked eggs or chopped ripe olives. If you want to garnish it, sprinkle with a few minced green onions or snipped chives.

Stir together thoroughly ¼ cup creamy Skippy peanut butter, ¼ cup chili sauce or catsup, ¼ cup chopped mango chutney, a dash of Tabasco (go easy), and salt and freshly ground black pepper to season.

Dr. MacLaughlin Special

You can buy tostadas or tortilla chips in a package. Cover each one with a little slice of good sharp Cheddar cheese. Open up a can of thawed frozen guacamole (avocado dip), and add a dash of Tabasco. Put the tostadas in a moderate oven until the cheese melts; while they're still hot, spoon some guacamole on the top and serve. And you've got the damnedest hors d'oeuvre you've ever put in your kisser.

SOUPS THAT AREN'T HOSPITAL SOUPS

Soup. What a helluva word and how much it covers—a cup of soup, a snack, a beginner to your meal, or it can be a meal in itself. In some parts of the world, soup is all there is. Gosh, you can make the stuff out of almost anything left over or start out fresh. Soups can be fish, meat, vegetable, fruit, hot, cold, mild, peppery, all kinds, even peanut butter.

Here are a few different soups. Some of them are great stick-to-your ribbers. Others are just fun.

Sour Cream Vichyssoise

Sometimes canned vichyssoise can be slippery, but this recipe makes it into a whole new thing.

It's OK to use frozen chopped chives.

1 can (13 ounces) vichyssoise, well chilled
½ cup commercial sour cream
Snipped fresh chives

Combine vichyssoise, sour cream, and 2 tablespoons chives in blender container, and whirl until smooth and fluffy. Pour into chilled cups, and sprinkle each serving with additional chives. Makes 4 first-course servings.

Caviar Vichyssoise

If a guy wants to show off on vichyssoise, he can do this for something fancy. Then he's really blowing his horn. But it's good.

Make your own vichyssoise by a good standard recipe and chill it well. Or use the canned kind. If you use the canned, chill it well and whirl it in a blender with a little heavy cream before you serve it. Pour chilled vichyssoise into soup cups. Top each serving with a generous sprinkling of snipped chives, a big spoonful of commercial sour cream, and a smaller spoonful of black or red caviar in the center of the sour cream.

Bongo Bongo Soup

Once in a while you create a dish, and you don't know whether it's gonna be accepted or forgotten. I made up this Bongo Bongo soup to replace a toheroa clam soup that we used to have on our restaurant menu—when we could no longer get those special clams from New Zealand due to World War II. Right off the bat, we had public acceptance of this soup. We've had just a lot of people eat this soup in our restaurants all over the world—in London, and Munich, and all over the United States.

2½ cups half and half (half milk, half cream)

10 ounces fresh oysters, poached (or 10 ounces drained canned oysters), whirled in a blender to purée

¼ cup strained creamed baby food spinach

2 tablespoons butter

1 small clove garlic, minced or mashed

½ teaspoon monosodium glutamate

About 1½ teaspoons A.1. sauce

About ½ teaspoon salt

About ⅜ teaspoon freshly ground black pepper

Generous dash of cayenne

2 teaspoons cornstarch mixed with 2 teaspoons cold water

About ⅔ cup heavy cream, whipped

In a large saucepan, heat half and half just to simmering. Add oyster purée, spinach, butter, garlic, monosodium glutamate, A.1. sauce, salt, pepper, and cayenne. Heat to simmering, whisking until smooth; do not boil. Add cornstarch mixture, and heat and whisk until soup is slightly thickened. Correct seasoning. Ladle into heatproof serving bowls. Top each with a spoonful of whipped cream. Slip under broiler until cream is well glazed with brown. Makes about 4 servings.

Trader Vic's Carrot Soup

You can also chill this soup and serve it cold. Be sure that the chicken broth you use is not salty.

3 cans (about 14 ounces each)
  or 5¼ cups chicken broth
¾ cup water
1 tablespoon instant minced
  dried onions
¼ teaspoon ground nutmeg
6 carrots, peeled and very
  thinly sliced

4 tablespoons heavy (whipping)
  cream
1½ tablespoons creamy peanut
  butter
About 2 teaspoons
  Worcestershire sauce
Generous dash of Tabasco
Commercial sour cream

Combine broth, water, onions, nutmeg, and carrots in a kettle. Cover and gently boil until carrots are very tender. Turn into blender container, and whirl until smooth. Add cream, peanut butter, Worcestershire, and Tabasco. Whirl again. Reheat if necessary. At serving time, pour into bowls or mugs, and top each serving with a spoonful of sour cream and a sprinkling of nutmeg. Makes 4 servings.

Yee Foo Mein

This is a noodle dish, so don't have too much broth in it—just enough so that the noodles can float around and heat up.

Now if you happen to have a few water chestnuts or bamboo shoots, put them into the broth; if you don't have any, OK. If you have some leftover roast chicken or half a squab, chop up the meat and add it to the broth; but it isn't necessary.

You can get fried egg noodles in packages in Chinatown; sometimes they're labeled *"yee foo mein."*

Cook a generous amount of noodles in plenty of boiling water just until they're limp, about 3 minutes. Drain. Heat some canned chicken broth along with some thinly sliced green onions with part of green tops (and water chestnuts, bamboo shoots, chicken, or squab if you have them) until boiling. Add the noodles and heat them up. Taste, and if the dish needs a little salt, add soy sauce instead. Pass soy.

Tortilla Soup

This can be a full meal soup.

1 pound boneless beef for boiling such as short ribs, brisket, or bottom round
4 frying chicken thighs
2 stalks celery
2 whole carrots, peeled
1 medium-sized onion, thinly sliced
1 bay leaf
1 whole clove
Salt
Water
1 large fresh or canned tomato, peeled, seeded, and diced

½ cup finely chopped fresh parsley
¼ cup finely chopped fresh cilantro (fresh coriander or Chinese parsley)
6 corn tortillas (each about 7 inches in diameter), cut into ¾-inch squares
½ cup grated or shredded Parmesan cheese
Freshly ground black pepper
Chili powder

Combine in a large kettle the beef, chicken, celery, carrots, onion, bay leaf, clove, 2 teaspoons salt, and 2 quarts water. Heat to boiling, then cover and simmer until chicken is tender, about 1 hour. Remove chicken, celery, and carrots. Remove chicken from bones, and tear into julienne strips. Cut celery and carrots into julienne strips. Meantime, continue to simmer beef until it is tender, adding more water if necessary in order to finish with 1½ quarts of liquid. Remove beef, and tear or cut into julienne strips. Remove bay leaf and clove from liquid. Put beef, chicken, celery, carrots, tomatoes, parsley, cilantro, and half of the tortillas into a serving casserole. If necessary, skim liquid in kettle. Add to casserole the liquid and onion from kettle. Season to taste with salt, pepper, and chili powder (about 2 teaspoons). Sprinkle with remaining tortillas. Sprinkle with Parmesan. Bake in a 400° oven until cheese melts, about 4 minutes. Sprinkle top lightly with additional chili powder. Makes 6 servings.

Matzo Ball Soup

Jewish cooks do a matzo ball soup. Sounds crazy, but it's terrific.

Make a clear chicken broth or a beef consommé. The matzo balls are easy to make. Here's the recipe. You make 'em look fancy by putting some chopped parsley in. Drop them into the hot broth.

Matzo balls   Beat 2 eggs with 2 tablespoons cold water and about ½ teaspoon salt. Stir in enough unsalted matzo meal to make a soft dough (about ½ cup) and 1 tablespoon minced fresh parsley. Chill for several hours. Shape into 12 small balls. Drop into boiling water, cover, and simmer for 20 minutes. Drain.

Trader Vic's Own Soup

My mother made a leek soup, *soupe au poireau*. It was a soup she made when we didn't feel good. She made it with chicken broth and leeks and potatoes and butter and egg—no thickening. You can still make it with leeks, but I prefer green onions. And look, don't monkey around making chicken broth. Use canned broth and you can make the whole soup in minutes.

Without the butter and potatoes, this soup is called Egg Flower Soup in Chinese cookery. So mine is really Egg Flower Soup, French style.

The butter makes it a little bit greasy and makes it taste good. You just drop in the onions during the last couple of minutes, so they're almost raw; they give a nice flavor. Last of all, you add the egg. Use only one egg for this amount of soup. Geez, if you use more, you're liable to make it as thick as mush.

Be sure your chicken broth isn't too salty.

4 cups chicken broth
¾ cup finely diced potatoes
½ cup ground raw chicken
  meat
2 tablespoons butter

⅓ cup minced green onions
  with part of green tops
Salt and freshly ground black
  pepper
1 egg, beaten

In a kettle, heat chicken broth to boiling. Add potatoes, cover, and gently boil until tender, about 10 minutes. Stir in chicken and butter, and cook for about 1 minute. Add onions and cook for 1 minute more. Season with salt and pepper. Slowly whisking, gradually trickle egg into simmering soup. Remove from heat and serve immediately. Makes 4 to 6 servings.

Peanut Soup

This peanut butter soup takes the cake. It's different, it causes comment, and it's easy to make.

½ cup finely chopped onions
½ cup finely chopped celery
¼ cup butter
3 cups chicken broth
1 cup creamy peanut butter

Dash of Tabasco
2 cups milk, scalded
About 1 teaspoon lemon juice
About ½ teaspoon celery salt
Parsley sprigs

In a kettle, sauté onions and celery in butter until limp. Add broth, cover, and gently boil until vegetables are very tender. Turn into blender container, add peanut butter and Tabasco, and whirl until smooth. Return to kettle, add milk, and reheat over low heat. Season with lemon juice and celery salt. Float a small parsley sprig on top of each serving. Makes 6 servings.

FISH LET'S MURDER SOME FISH RECIPES

Fish takes the biggest beating of all the things we cook. Damn few people and damn few restaurants can cook a piece of fish properly. And it's really the easiest thing to do. And you can do more nice things with fish than with any other food.

Most people overcook fish. All you ever need to do is to cook a fish just until the flesh flakes with a fork. Don't do more. And with shellfish, you just cook it until it is cooked through to the center, opaque throughout. One exception is catfish; you fry the hell out of them.

FRYING FISH

Most people seem to think that you have to brown fish to make it look good. Well, hell, I guess you have to look at it, but most of all, you want to eat it. And it is almost impossible to fry fish enough to get some brown color on it before it's too well done and not fit to eat. Things like salmon, trout, sole—you hardly fry 'em.

POACHING FISH

Here's my rule for fish where the flesh is about an inch thick. Heat your particular stock to a rolling boil, then slide the fish into it. The stock will stop boiling because the fish has cooled it down. Then bring the stock up to a boil, and shut off the fire. Let the fish stand in the stock for a few minutes until the heat goes through it. That's all. It will be tender, wonderful, full of flavor, and the absolute most.

Now if you have a great big thick piece of fish, let it simmer for maybe a minute, then shut off the heat. But don't go overdoing the cooking.

USING CANNED OR FROZEN COOKED FISH

All this fish or shellfish—such as clams, shrimp, lobster, salmon —is cooked already when you get it. So don't cook it over again; simply bring it to the heat. Don't go cooking the hell out of it or you'll destroy what little flavor you have to start with.

Trader Vic Frog's Legs

There's only one way to do frog's legs, and this is it.

Lightly salt and pepper and flour the frog's legs, and fry in butter until cooked and golden brown. Separately, sauté chopped shallots and very finely sliced mushrooms in a little butter. Add a little light dry white wine and cook it enough to reduce the alcohol. Then add a lot of butter to the shallots and melt it down *just* until it's creamy, not down to a liquid. Put the frog's legs on a plate, pour this creamy shallot butter sauce down over them, just lift and shake the legs a little to let the sauce roll down over the legs.

Sunflower Sole

¼ cup shelled raw sunflower
    seeds
1 cup chicken broth
⅓ cup butter
2 tablespoons minced green
    onions with part of green tops
⅓ cup dry white table wine
1¼ teaspoons Trader Vic's
    Javanese Saté Spice

1 teaspoon seasoning salt
4 sole fillets (about 1¼ pounds
    total)
2 tablespoons fresh lemon juice
1 cup heavy (whipping) cream
Finely chopped fresh parsley

Cover sunflower seeds with water, heat to boiling, remove from heat and let stand for 10 minutes, drain well. Combine seeds and broth in a small saucepan, cover, and simmer for 10 minutes. Melt butter in a wide, heavy frying pan. Add onions, wine, saté spice, and seasoning salt. Fold each fillet in half, crosswise, and arrange in the pan, spooning liquid over. Cover pan with foil. Bake in a 325° oven just until fish loses translucency and begins to flake with a fork, about 15 minutes. With a slotted spatula, lift fish, drain well, and place on warm serving plates or platter; keep warm. Drain broth from sunflower seeds, add to frying pan, and cook liquid in pan over high heat until reduced to about ¾ cup. Add seeds, lemon juice, and all except 3 tablespoons of the cream and cook over high heat, stirring, until liquid is reduced to consistency of heavy cream. Whip remaining cream, and fold in. Turn sauce over sole. Sprinkle generously with parsley. Makes 4 servings.

Poached Salmon in Red Caviar Sauce

You eat the red caviar with the red salmon, and it's just a symphony.

Court bouillon (recipe below)
4 pieces salmon fillet, each about
    ½ pound
1 cup dry white table wine
4 tablespoons butter
2 teaspoons fresh lemon juice

2 cups heavy (whipping) cream
2 egg yolks
4 tablespoons red caviar
Salt and freshly ground black
    pepper
4 thin lemon slices

Prepare court bouillon. Slip fillets into bubbling bouillon. Heat until bouillon returns to a boil. Turn off heat, and allow salmon to rest over burner with the heat off until it barely flakes with a fork. The salmon should be cooked just enough and not be overcooked. In a wide, shallow pan, combine 1 cup of the poaching broth, the wine, and butter. Cook over high heat until reduced by half. Add lemon juice and all except 4 tablespoons of the cream. Cook over high heat, stirring, until blended and slightly reduced to the consistency of cream. Remove from heat. Beat a little of the sauce into egg yolks. Gradually whisk egg yolk mixture back into sauce. Whip remaining cream, and fold in along with 2 tablespoons of the caviar. Correct seasoning with a little salt (the garnishing caviar is salty) and with pepper if you wish. With a slotted spatula, lift fish from bouillon, drain well, and place on warm serving plates. Pour sauce over. Center each fillet with a lemon slice and a spoonful of caviar. Makes 4 servings.

Court bouillon   Combine in a wide frying pan 6 cups water; 1 onion, sliced; 1 whole lemon, sliced; 2 stalks celery with leaves; 1 large bay leaf; 6 whole allspice; 6 whole peppercorns; and ½ teaspoon salt. Cover, bring to a boil, then gently boil for 5 minutes.

Chilled Caviar Salmon with Mustard Dressing

You can do nearly the same thing with cold salmon. This is pretty, too; looks like a million dollars.

Poach the fish as I told you, and chill it. Then serve it on a bed of salad greens with a liberal amount of Wasabi Dressing (recipe page 91) or Mustard Dressing (page 92) spooned over, a thin lemon slice on that, and a gob of red caviar on that.

Cracked Crab, Chinese Style

Take a couple of freshly cooked (still hot) and cleaned Dungeness crabs. Crack them: crack all the claws, and make each belly part into about 6 pieces. Take the crab backs and scoop out all the butter—the fat yellow stuff that's clinging to the shell; reserve that. In a big pot, melt ½ cup of butter. Stir in the crab butter, dry French vermouth (about 6 tablespoons), 2 big cloves of mashed garlic, and salt (about ½ teaspoon), pepper (about ¼ teaspoon freshly ground), and Worcestershire (about ½ teaspoon) to taste. Heat and stir all that together. Then put in the crab, and mix it around and keep turning it around in the sauce until it is hot. Heat it up well. That's it. Eat it with your fingers. And that's the best thing you've ever put into your cotton pickin' mouth. If you want more sauce, double the butter, vermouth, and seasonings. Makes 2 to 4 servings.

Deviled Crab

½ cup minced fresh onions
½ cup butter
⅓ cup flour
About 1 tablespoon dry mustard
2 cups milk
About 1 tablespoon
  Worcestershire sauce
Dash of Tabasco
1 tablespoon minced fresh
  parsley

½ pound flaked crab meat
Salt and freshly ground black
  pepper
4 large crab legs, shelled
3 tablespoons grated or shredded
  Parmesan cheese
Paprika

In a heavy saucepan or frying pan, sauté onions in 6 tablespoons of the butter until very tender. Add flour and mustard and cook and stir to make a smooth paste. Gradually add milk, cooking and stirring over medium heat to make a smooth and thickened sauce. Simmer, stirring, for 5 minutes more. Stir in Worchestershire, Tabasco, and 2 teaspoons of the parsley. Fold in flaked crab meat. Correct seasoning with salt and pepper. Pile into 2 buttered shell (or other individual) baking dishes. Arrange 2 crab legs on top of each. Sprinkle with Parmesan and dust with paprika. Melt remaining butter and pour over top. Bake in a 400° oven until heated through and golden brown on top, about 10 minutes. Sprinkle with remaining parsley. Makes 2 servings.

Fisherman's Spaghetti

My bride and I once took a day's ride down from Rome to a place called Amalfi. We arrived about lunchtime, and our driver took us to a fish joint on the waterfront. If you go to Rome, you really should take the ride. It's beautiful—crazy road, lots of goofy Italians driving like mad—oh boy, you'll stay awake!

Well, anyhow, the waiter in this joint suggests "Special Spaghetti" with some damn sauce thing which turns out to be clams, shrimp, and various other kinds of shellfish. Well, I ate till I popped. So I came home and created Fisherman's Spaghetti.

I like this as well as or better than the Amalfi version, and this is so quick and easy to make. Open the cans, boil the spaghetti, and you're eating in less than a half hour. Complete the meal with a green salad and some white wine.

½ cup minced fresh onions
½ cup butter
⅔ cup dry white table wine
1 can (10½ ounces) Aunt Penny's white sauce
2 cloves garlic, minced or mashed
2 or 3 dashes Tabasco sauce
1 can (1 pound) whole clams
1 can (8 ounces) minced clams
1 can (4½ ounces) small shrimp

1 can (about 7 ounces) Dungeness crab meat
Salt and freshly ground black pepper
About 12 ounces dry or 1½ pounds fresh spaghetti, cooked in boiling salted water until just tender (al dente) and drained
Grated Parmesan cheese
Finely chopped fresh parsley

In a large frying pan, sauté onions in half of the butter until tender. Add wine and cook, stirring, until wine is reduced by half. Stir in white sauce, remaining butter, garlic, and Tabasco. Add whole clams, minced clams, shrimp, and crab (all shellfish with their juices). Heat and gently turn until sauce is bubbling and blended. Add pepper to taste and salt if you need it. Arrange hot spaghetti on a deep platter, pour shellfish sauce over, and sprinkle generously with Parmesan and lightly with parsley. Makes about 6 servings.

Prawns, San Francisco Style

Shellfish, San Francisco Style, is a thing we started in our San Francisco restaurant to show a particular style of cooking any shellfish. Try it, you'll like it.

Danish scampi make this dish outstanding. I don't know where we first discovered the little critters, but they are good. First of all, I can tell you that they didn't come from the sewers of some large city, but were harvested in the deep, clear waters off Iceland. They are absolutely unique so far as scampi are concerned. Now one thing for sure: don't overcook these little babies because they can get like pencil rubbers in a few minutes. Cook them *just* until they lose their translucency.

Since you can't often get Danish or Icelandic scampi in your market, you can use this same recipe and use shelled and deveined prawns or shrimp—from 1½ to 4 inches long. Just cook your prawns according to what you have, always just until they lose translucency; and that's almost nothing for little ones, a few minutes for bigger ones.

1½ pounds raw prawns	**1½ cups heavy (whipping)**
6 tablespoons butter	**cream**
Salt and freshly ground black	**⅓ cup Hollandaise Sauce**
pepper	**(recipe page 44)**
4 tablespoons minced shallots	**Croutons (recipe below)**
½ cup dry white table wine	**Minced fresh parsley**

Shell and devein prawns. In a frying pan over medium heat, sauté prawns in about 4 tablespoons of the butter just until they turn pink and firm and lose translucence. Season lightly with salt and pepper. Meantime, in a wide frying pan, sauté shallots in 2 tablespoons butter just until heated through. Add wine and cook until wine reduces by half. Add cream and cook, stirring, until liquid is reduced to consistency of heavy cream. Add prawns and turn to blend. Remove from heat and fold in Hollandaise. Sprinkle with croutons and a little parsley. Makes 4 servings.

Croutons. Trim crusts off French bread slices and cut into cubes no larger than ½ inch on a side; measure 1 cup. In a frying pan over medium heat, sauté cubes in about 2 tablespoons butter until crisp and brown.

Trader Vic's Two Ways with Mussels

Scrape barnacles off mussels, then scrub mussels with a stiff brush under running water. Put equal parts of enough dry white table wine and water in bottom of a kettle to reach a depth of about

¼ inch. Add a clove or two of garlic, crushed, and a small handful of chopped fresh parsley. Heat to boiling. Add cleaned mussels. Cover and simmer for about 5 minutes or until the shells open. Remove and discard one half of the shell from each mussel. With a scissors, trim off the beard of each mussel. Arrange mussels, open side up, in serving plates.

1 Strain the broth and serve in small cups to sip. Make this sauce: Melt butter just so it is creamy—not down to a liquid—and stir in just a little A.1. sauce to season. Dip mussels into the sauce before eating.

2 Strain the broth. Cook, uncovered, over high until it reduces to about 1½ tablespoons. Stir into about ½ cup Hollandaise Sauce (1 recipe below). Spoon sauce over cooked mussels.

Blender Hollandaise

Put 3 egg yolks, 2 tablespoons fresh lemon juice, ¼ teaspoon salt, and a dash of Tabasco in blender container. Heat ½ cup butter until it bubbles; do not brown. Turn blender on high speed, and immediately pour in hot butter in a steady stream through small opening in blender cover. Add ½ teaspoon Dijon-style mustard, and whirl until blended, about 15 seconds. Makes ¾ to 1 cup sauce.

Note: To reheat any remaining sauce for later use, place in top part of double boiler over hot (not boiling) water; stir until smooth and warm.

Trader Vic Gumbo

There are all kinds of crazy recipes for a New Orleans gumbo. There are all kinds of gumbo. Mine most likely won't be like every other gumbo, but it is one helluva dish. I used to cook this at my hunting club when we had ten or twelve to feed. I'd make a great big pot of this stuff.

Now don't cook the gumbo filé too much or you'll destroy the flavor. Add it just before the fish, and serve the dish immediately when the fish is just poached through.

6 frying chicken drumsticks
Salt and freshly ground black
  pepper
Butter
2 medium-sized onions, finely
  chopped
1 cup chopped celery
⅓ cup finely chopped fresh
  parsley
2 cups chicken broth
¾ cup dry white table wine
1 large can (1 pound 12 ounces)
  peeled whole tomatoes
  (preferably Italian pear-
  shaped tomatoes), broken up

Dash of Tabasco
2 large cloves garlic, minced
  or mashed
About 2 tablespoons gumbo filé
1½ pounds fillets of rock cod,
  red snapper, sea bass, or
  other firm-fleshed white sea
  fish, cut into 1½-inch squares
2 medium-sized freshly cooked,
  cleaned, and cracked
  Dungeness crabs (or ¾ to 1
  pound large pieces of shelled
  crab meat)
½ pound cooked and shelled
  tiny shrimp

Season chicken well with salt and pepper. In a large, heavy kettle over medium heat, brown chicken well in about 3 tablespoons butter. Remove chicken. Add to kettle enough more butter to make 4 tablespoons. Add onions and celery, and sauté until limp. Stir in 4 tablespoons of the parsley, the broth, wine, tomatoes, Tabasco, and garlic. Return chicken to kettle. Cover and simmer until chicken is very tender, about 50 minutes, stirring occasionally. Stir in 2 tablespoons gumbo filé. Add fish, crab, and shrimp, and simmer just until fish flakes with a fork, about 5 minutes. Taste and add salt, pepper, and additional gumbo filé to season well. Ladle into soup plates. Sprinkle with remaining parsley. Makes 6 servings.

Macadamia Parmesan Sole

½ cup soft butter
½ cup shredded or grated
  Parmesan cheese
4 sole fillets (about 1½ pounds
  total)

½ cup finely chopped
  macadamia nuts
Watercress or parsley sprigs
Freshly ground black pepper

Spread half of the butter thickly over bottom of a shallow baking pan. Sprinkle with half of the Parmesan. Wipe sole dry with a damp cloth, and arrange in a single layer over cheese. Dot sole with remaining butter, sprinkle with remaining Parmesan and with the macadamias. Bake in a 400° oven, basting occasionally with melted butter and cheese, for 15 minutes or until fish just flakes with a fork and butter and nuts are brown and crusty. Serve with pan drippings spooned over sole. Garnish with watercress. Pass black pepper, and grind on lightly. Makes 4 servings.

Baked Striped Bass My Mother's Way

You can use this method for cooking any solid, firm-fleshed fish such as red snapper or rock cod. I wouldn't do it with salmon.

My mother did it two ways, and I'll tell you both of them.

1 Take a baking pan big enough so that the fish will fit into it. Cover the bottom of the pan with a liberal amount of finely chopped onions and finely chopped celery. Season them lightly with salt and pepper. Sprinkle very lightly with fine dried bread crumbs. Stud it generously with pieces of butter. Sprinkle the cavity of the whole striped bass (usually about 4 to 6 pounds), cleaned and head removed, with salt and pepper. Place fish on bed of celery and onions. Then do the same thing to the top of the fish: cover it with loads of very finely chopped celery and onions, a little salt and pepper, then a few bread crumbs, then dot well with butter. Mix together a cup of white wine, a cup of water, and a couple of dashes of Tabasco. Gently sprinkle that all over the fish until the crumbs are saturated. Now don't dump it all over the fish at once and wash off all the crumbs. Then pour enough of the wine-water mixture into the bottom of the pan to make it ½ inch deep. Mix up some more if you need to. Then bake in a 350° oven for about 40 minutes to 1 hour, depending upon the size of the fish—until the fish flakes with a fork. Baste the fish occasionally during baking with the juices in the pan; use that same light sprinkling action as before. Serve the fish with the pan juices as a sauce.

2 Follow the same procedure as above *except* add a few chopped canned tomatoes and a little chopped green bell pepper next to the fish on both sides. I like this better than the other way.

Salmon Croquettes

Gosh, when I was a kid, my mom and pop had a little grocery store, and canned salmon was twenty-five cents a can. Mom would use a can to make salmon croquettes (fresh salmon was too hard to come by).

Sometimes I still make them at home, and sit there and eat them and think about what a wonderful world it was when I was ten or twelve years old. That was a thousand years ago, and it's still a great place!

I like these just plain with some lemon juice to squeeze on. But you can serve them with a cream sauce.

¼ cup minced fresh onions
Butter
1 small can (about 8 ounces) salmon
⅓ to ½ cup mashed potatoes
1 egg, lightly beaten
Salt and freshly ground black pepper

Sauté onions in about 2 tablespoons butter until limp. Drain salmon, remove skin and large bones, and flake the meat. Lightly mix together the salmon, onions, potatoes, egg, and enough salt and pepper to season well. For each croquette, lightly shape about ¼ cup of the mixture into a patty about 3 inches in diameter. In a heavy frying pan over medium heat, fry patties in a generous amount of butter until brown and crisp on both sides. Makes about 5 croquettes.

Alaska King Crab, Mai Tai Style

If you need a quick fish course, you can make this one from frozen Alaska crab legs. Smaller servings also make a nice dish to please your little sweetie as a first course.

8 shelled Alaska king crab legs (3½ to 4 ounces each)
Salt and freshly ground black pepper
4 teaspoons Dijon-style mustard
½ cup half and half (half milk and half cream)
Fine cracker crumbs
About 5 tablespoons butter
2 small limes
4 thin lime slices
Finely chopped fresh parsley

Cut each crab leg in half lengthwise. Season with salt and pepper. Spread evenly with mustard. Lightly dip into half and half to moisten, then dip into cracker crumbs just to coat slightly. Melt butter over medium heat in a frying pan. Add crab legs, and sauté until golden on both sides. Arrange crab legs on serving plate. Heat butter remaining in frying pan over higher heat until it bubbles and browns (add a little more butter if necessary). Spoon over crab. Squeeze on lime juice. Garnish with lime slices and sprinkle with parsley. Makes 4 servings.

Crayfish Bisque

It's an awful nice thing to make a crayfish bisque, but it's just a lot of trouble—the way I make it, anyway. This is not a hurry-up dish. But if you've got a lot of crayfish and a lot of friends, it's not too hard.

Get your crayfish—nice and fresh and alive. Get a big pot and put in white wine and water (half and half), some garlic, some celery stalks and some quartered onions. Bring it to a boil. Then put in your crayfish and cook those little kids in there until they're pink and done. Then scoop them out of the broth and let them cool off.

Separate out the little crayfish that are too little to fool with and put them in a cheesecloth bag. Now with the big ones: Take off their heads, take out the fat and guck in the heads and put it into the cheesecloth bag. Break off their claws and put them into the bag. Save the head shells and save the meaty tails. Get the guests shelling and cleaning the big tails until you've got a lot of meat. Make a stuffing to fill the heads: If you're cooking for about 10 people: Take about 1½ cups of the shelled crayfish tails. Put 'em in a blender with 1 small can of drained Louisiana shrimp, a little thick fresh cream, 1 egg, salt and pepper, and a little bourbon whisky. Grind it all up to make a thick and tasty paste. Stuff the heads with that.

Now take the celery and onions out of the pot and put 'em in the bag with the claws and little crayfish and guck. Tie it up and pound it and mash it up with a hammer or a bottle until it's all mushy. Put this into the pot with the broth. Heat the broth in the pot to boiling, add the stuffed heads, and poach them in the gently boiling broth for about 10 minutes. Lift them out.

Now start to make the reduction of the broth. Cook it down, down, down until you have a nice strong broth. Take the cheese-cloth bag out of the broth and squeeze out all the juice into the broth. Take some thick cream—at least a pint—bring it to a boil, pour it into the broth. Then thicken the whole thing with a little *roux* (whisk in a paste of equal flour and soft butter and cook, whisking, until liquid is smooth and thickened). Add about a teaspoon of paprika to make it nice and pink—not too pink, just slightly pink.

Put the stuffed heads in there and the remaining big crayfish tails and just heat through to warm it all up. The stuffed choice big heads float on top and you suck those, and spoon up the soup. And that's the best thing you've ever put in your cotton pickin' lips.

Oh-So-Good Peachy POULTRY Recipes

Chicken and such stuff seem to have lost a lot of status in our society dining these days—mainly, I guess, because it's so much trouble to get the meat off the bones. Many people think that it's terribly ill mannered to pick up a drumstick with your fingers. Frankly, I don't give a tinker's damn about all this etiquette crap. I like to thoroughly enjoy what I'm eating, fingers or no fingers.

Chicken for one is a cheap meat. Because it's cheap is no reason why it can't be fantastic.

In this chapter, you'll find things that you can do with fowl that are unique and terribly good. You'll find a couple more chicken recipes in the Pomp and Splendor chapter.

Sunflower Chicken

Geez, my old lady handed me some raw sunflower seeds one day a couple of months ago. They were just like chewing nails. But they tasted good. So I said to myself, "Why can't we boil these and make them tender?" So I boiled them. And they're the damnedest things you ever ate.

So then I made them into a sauce for chicken. Here's the recipe. On page 39, there's my recipe for them with fish. And on page 95, there's my recipe for them in a bean sprout salad.

1 cup dry white table wine
2 tablespoons fresh lemon juice
1¼ teaspoons Trader Vic's Javanese Saté Spice
1 teaspoon seasoning salt
2 whole large chicken breasts, split, boned, and skinned if you wish (4 breast pieces)

⅓ cup shelled raw sunflower seeds
1 cup chicken broth
3 tablespoons butter
1 cup heavy (whipping) cream
Salt and freshly ground black pepper
Finely chopped fresh parsley

Combine wine, lemon juice, saté spice, and seasoning salt. Add chicken, and let marinate for 30 minutes. Cover sunflower seeds with water, heat to boiling, remove from heat and let stand for 10 minutes, drain well. Combine sunflower seeds and broth in a small saucepan, cover, and simmer for 10 minutes. Remove chicken from marinade, pat dry, and save marinade. In a heavy frying pan over medium heat, brown chicken on all sides in butter, about 10 minutes total. Add marinade. Cover and cook over low heat just until chicken loses translucency and is tender, about 10 minutes. Remove chicken to warm serving plates or platter; keep warm. Drain broth from sunflower seeds and add to frying pan. Cook liquid in pan over high heat until reduced to about ¾ cup. Add all of the cream except 3 tablespoons and cook over high heat, stirring, until liquid is reduced to consistency of heavy cream. Stir in sunflower seeds. Taste and correct seasoning with salt and pepper. Whip remaining cream, and fold in. Spoon sauce over chicken. Sprinkle generously with parsley. Makes 4 servings.

Chicken and Dumplings

This chicken and dumpling dish is really something.

First of all, don't get an old chicken; it's still old after you've boiled it for five hours. Get a young chicken.

3½-pound chicken, cut into
  pieces
4 cups water
1 teaspoon salt
⅛ teaspoon monosodium
  glutamate
10 whole black peppercorns
1 stalk celery with leaves
1 parsley sprig
1 onion, peeled and quartered
1 bay leaf

3 tablespoons flour mixed with
  3 tablespoons cold water
3 carrots
1 cup thinly sliced celery
Pinch of ground nutmeg
  (optional)
Salt and freshly ground black
  pepper
Dumplings (recipe page 113)
Finely chopped fresh parsley

Put into a kettle chicken, water, salt, monosodium glutamate, peppercorns, celery stalk, parsley sprig, onion, and bay leaf. Cover, heat to boiling, then simmer until meat is very tender, about 1 hour. Lift chicken from broth. Discard skin and bones, and break meat into large pieces. Strain broth, return to kettle, and heat to bubbling. Stirring constantly, gradually add flour-water mixture to bubbling liquid in kettle. Cook and stir until slightly thickened. Add chicken, carrots, celery, and nutmeg if you wish. Taste and correct seasoning with salt and pepper. Make the dumpling dough and drop by heaping spoonfuls (making 8 dumplings), onto gently bubbling liquid. Cover kettle tightly, and cook for 40 minutes (do not lift cover; keep liquid gently bubbling). Lift dumplings from liquid, and arrange as a border around a warm, deep serving platter. Turn chicken into center of platter. Sprinkle with chopped parsley. Makes 4 servings.

Easy Chicken Fricassee with Polenta

3-pound frying chicken, cut into
serving pieces
Salt and freshly ground black
pepper
Flour
About 2 tablespoons butter
About 2 tablespoons salad oil
1 can (14 ounces) chicken broth
1 tablespoon flour stirred until
smooth with 1 tablespoon cold
water
Worcestershire sauce to taste
(about 1 to 1½ teaspoons)

Dash of Tabasco
1 small can (8 ounces) sliced
carrots, drained
1 small can (8 ounces) small
potatoes, drained
1 small can (8 ounces) small
boiling onions, drained
⅓ cup pitted ripe olives
(preferably Greek olives),
sliced
Cheese polenta (½ recipe page
114)
Finely chopped fresh parsley

Season chicken with salt and pepper and dust with flour. In a heavy kettle over medium-high heat, brown chicken on all sides in butter and salad oil. Remove any excess grease; leave brown drippings. Add broth. Cover and simmer until chicken is very tender, about 45 minutes. Remove chicken. Heat liquid in kettle to bubbling. Gradually whisk in flour-water paste. Heat and stir until liquid is slightly thickened and smooth; then simmer, stirring, for about 3 minutes more. Stir in Worcestershire, Tabasco, and salt and pepper to season. Return chicken to kettle along with carrots, potatoes, onions, and olives. Heat through. Serve over cheese polenta. Sprinkle with parsley. Makes 4 servings.

Malay Peanut Chicken

The sweet red ginger is essential—no substitutes. It comes in jars. You buy it in Chinese or specialty food stores.

Just multiply if you want more servings.

1 whole large chicken breast, split, boned, and skinned (2 breast pieces)
1½ teaspoons Kikkoman soy sauce
Salt and freshly ground black pepper
Flour
1½ tablespoons butter
1 tablespoon minced green onions with part of green tops
⅔ cup chicken broth
¼ cup dry white table wine
2 tablespoons chunk-style peanut butter
½ teaspoon ground turmeric
1 teaspoon rinsed and drained minced Chinese sweet red ginger
⅓ cup heavy (whipping) cream
2 teaspoons finely chopped salted roasted peanuts

Moisten breast surfaces with ½ teaspoon of the soy sauce. Season lightly with salt and pepper, and dust with flour. In a heavy frying pan over medium heat, brown breasts on both sides in butter, about 10 minutes total. Stir onions into drippings. Add broth, wine, peanut butter, turmeric, ginger, and remaining soy. Stir to blend. Cover and cook over low heat just until chicken loses translucency and is tender, about 10 minutes. Remove chicken to warm serving platter or plates. Add cream to juices in pan. Cook and stir over high heat until liquid reduces to thin sauce consistency. Correct seasoning with salt and pepper. Pour sauce over chicken. Sprinkle with peanuts. Makes 1 or 2 servings.

Paprika Chicken Breasts

Paprika Chicken, and I don't mean Paprika Hungarian Style. I mean like Paprika Stroganoff Style—julienne of chicken.

You can put it with rice. Or you can go down to the store and get a package of Knorr *spaetzle* and make it up like it says on the package. Serve the chicken with rice or buttered spaetzle and you've got a heck of a meal.

2 whole large chicken breasts,
  boned and skinned (1 pound
  of boned meat)
1½ tablespoons flour
Salt and freshly ground black
  pepper
About 3 tablespoons butter
4 teaspoons minced shallots
½ pound fresh mushrooms,
  thinly sliced
½ cup dry white table wine
2 teaspoons paprika
1½ cups commercial sour cream
1 tablespoon Worcestershire
  sauce
Chopped watercress leaves and
  watercress sprigs

Slice chicken into strips about 3 inches by ½ inch. Combine flour, ½ teaspoon salt, and ¼ teaspoon pepper in a clean paper bag. Add chicken, and shake to coat. In a large frying pan, sauté chicken in butter over medium-high heat just until opague throughout and tender. Remove from pan and keep warm. Add shallots, mushrooms, and wine to frying pan, and cook, stirring until liquid reduces to about 2 tablespoons. Reduce heat to low. Stir in paprika. Stir in sour cream and Worcestershire. Fold in chicken, heat through, and season generously with salt and lightly with pepper. Sprinkle generously with chopped watercress. Garnish with watercress sprigs. Makes 4 servings.

Chicken Dali Dali

We don't begin to use enough fruit in our cooking and it's great. A good thing with this is Rice Roberta, page 117.

2 whole large chicken breasts,
  split and boned (4 breast
  pieces)
Salt and freshly ground black
  pepper
About ¼ cup butter
2 tablespoons minced green
  onions with part of green tops
1 cup chicken broth
2 slightly underripe bananas,
  peeled and halved lengthwise
1 slightly underripe papaya,
  peeled, seeded, and cut into
  12 lengthwise slices
4 lengthwise slices of fresh
  pineapple, each about ½ inch
  thick
2 teaspoons fresh lemon juice

Sprinkle chicken generously with salt and with pepper to season. Melt about 2 tablespoons of the butter in a heavy frying pan over medium heat. Add chicken, and brown on both sides, about 10

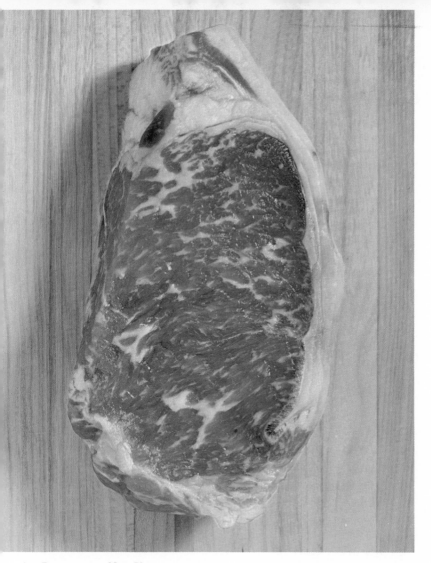

1. PICTURED ARE NEW YORK CUT STEAKS.

This first picture is of *prime* beef. On a prime animal, the piece of meat running along the rib cage and out to the skin is usually thick in diameter, and
it is a little shorter than with lesser cuts of beef. It is covered with a thick
layer of white (not yellow) fat. Fat marbles all the way through prime beef.
Fat is what makes the thing taste good. Of course, it still depends on the
individual animal—how much the damn thing ran around and how much fat
he ate—how tender the steak is going to be. When you get down to the nitty
gritty, the prime is not the best piece of meat to be putting into your body
because it has too damn much fat. But if you want to show off and pay five
or six bucks a piece, prime is what you'll use.

2. *Choice* is the piece of meat that most restaurants use. On a choice New York cut, the diameter of the meat from the bones out to the skin is not quite as thick as the prime. Choice has a little less fat marbling. This picture is of an exceptionally good quality piece of choice beef. It would really be just as tasty as the prime. If you had twenty steaks of each kind in front of you, you'd have a helluva time finding which was choice and which was prime.

3. Then you have the *good* quality piece, which is what I like to eat. In it, there is not much fat marbling, fewer calories, less cholesterol. If it is well aged, this is the piece of meat that you should put on your table.

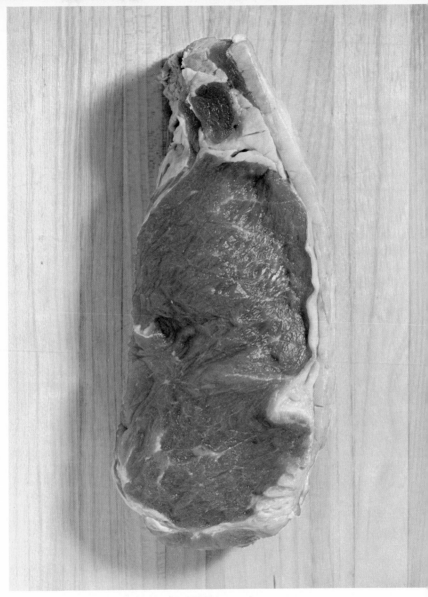

4.   The *utility* piece has more firmness. The big problem with this is to find
out how much the animal ran around; the meat could very likely be tough
and stringy. Or it could have come from a scrawny cow or an old bull that
never got fat. After all, remember what I told you, you can't make a silk
purse out of a sow's ear.

minutes total. Stir onions into butter. Add 2 tablespoons of the broth. Cover and cook over low heat just until chicken loses translucency and is tender, about 5 minutes. Remove chicken, onions, and any liquid to warm serving plates or platter; keep warm. Melt remaining butter over medium heat in same frying pan. Add fruit slices, and sauté on both sides just until heated through and golden. Arrange alongside chicken. Add remaining broth to frying pan and cook and stir over high heat, loosening drippings, until liquid reduces to about ½ cup. Stir in lemon juice. Pour over chicken and fruit. Makes 2 or 4 servings.

Corn Bread Stuffing for Turkey

We go fishing once in a while on the Madison River. And we stay in West Yellowstone at a little resort called the Parade Rest. It's run by Lu and Bud Morris. These kids are just down to earth, live in a little log cabin, and are as cute as hell. We eat family style, and it's good. One day, they cooked a turkey and stuffed it with the best stuffing ever. It's made out of corn bread.

Make your corn bread and let it age for three days. Then you can get an idea of whether or not you'll need an egg or two in the stuffing for added moistness and to bind. If you squeeze the corn bread in your hand and it has enough moisture to stick together, it is moist enough so the stuffing probably won't need egg. But if it crumbles dryly, it needs moisture, so add the egg or two and maybe a little chicken broth. If you like your stuffing really rich, add some more butter.

½ pound ground lean pork
½ pound ground chuck
½ cup butter
2 large onions, chopped
2 cups chopped celery
3 tablespoons Bell's poultry seasoning
1 large clove garlic, minced or mashed
About 2 teaspoons salt
About ½ teaspoon freshly ground black pepper
8 to 10 cups finely broken three-day-old corn bread
2 eggs, beaten
Warm chicken broth (optional)

In a large frying pan, slowly brown pork and beef in their own fat. When crumbly, add butter and melt. Add onions and celery and sauté until limp. Stir in poultry seasoning, garlic, salt, and pepper. Toss thoroughly with corn bread and eggs. (If you wish more moister stuffing, add a little broth.) Correct seasoning. Use as stuffing for turkey. Makes about 3 quarts.

GAME RECIPES
GOOD BAD INDIFFERENT

Oh, boy, I've been hunting since I was a kid of thirteen. And I know that there are a million ways to do everything right and wrong in cooking. Wild game is usually lousy, but you've killed it and now you have to eat it. You can either cook the hell out of it and then it'll be like any other tough meat cooked for a long time. Or you can nurse it along and it can be what it's supposed to be: wild game. —Pssst. Some of it can be good.

WILD DUCK

To me this is, without doubt, the best hunting and shooting bird of them all. I think that the best eating bird of all the ducks is a northern spooner which just came down from Canada, has been feeding on rice and grain, and is still very pink when you take the feathers off.

How long do you cook a duck? How long is a piece of string? But here's a general idea.

Soy-glazed Wild Duck Roast

This is what I like to do when roasting. You can use any kind of wild duck for this.

Wipe ducks dry. Rub ducks inside and out with Trader Vic's or Kikkoman soy sauce. Do this early in the day, and put the ducks in the refrigerator to let the soy dry. When it's time for dinner, put the birds on a rack in a roasting pan. To roast a mallard or a sprig, give it 18 minutes at 500°. Then you'll have pink duck.

Wild Duck Breasts and Duck Soup

This is the best way to cook duck for a mixed group. You can serve some choice breast pieces and then follow with a great dinner duck soup—because there is plenty of meat on the duck bones. With French bread, salad, and wine, this makes a great light meal.

Wild Duck Breasts

Take some big ducks, mallard or sprig. Bone out the breasts and take off the breast skin. Dip the whole breast pieces into soy sauce so they're well coated on both sides. Let stand for a few minutes, and dip them again and let the soy dry a little. Get a heavy frying pan hot over the fire, put a little grease in it, and fry those breasts for 4 minutes on each side, and serve. Believe me, kids, these'll be pink and *nice* if you have a good hot fire. Or you can grill them over charcoal just until pink. Good, good, good! Now with the carcasses from the ducks . . .

Duck Soup

You do this with the raw carcasses of the ducks after the breasts have been boned out. (Or you can use the carcasses of roast ducks—if you have them left after people have eaten just the breasts out of the ducks and left the meat and bones that they haven't chewed on). Brown the raw carcasses in a 500° oven.

Chop up the browned carcasses with a hatchet (or a cleaver; but hatchet sounds more like wild country style). Put the carcasses in a big pot with a glass of white wine, chopped onions, sliced carrots, sliced celery, mashed garlic, a bay leaf, salt and pepper, and a little pinch of thyme to season, and a quantity of pearl barley— maybe about ½ cup for 2 quarts of water—and water to cover it all. Cover and simmer until the meat and barley are very tender, about 2 hours. Remove meat from bones and put it back into the pot. Discard the bones. Correct seasoning. Believe me, duck soup is duck soup. It's good.

DOVES

Doves, Ranch Style

It used to be that every year we went down to Texas for a dove shoot. What fun and hospitality we always had! We'd have lunch out in the prairie under the wonderful Texas oaks. The doves we'd shot that morning would be cooked for lunch—sometimes one way, sometimes another way, but always only one of two ways.

First way Season the cleaned birds with salt and pepper and spiral-wrap each in thinly sliced bacon. Then barbecue over a hot fire for 10 minutes.

The other way, simple Split the cleaned doves down the back to flatten them. Season on both sides with salt and pepper. Grill them over a hot charcoal fire for 7 to 10 minutes.

Doves, John Metcalf Style

Wipe cleaned doves dry. Season them lightly inside and out with salt and pepper. Rub a little marjoram or rosemary into the cavities. Fry them in a generous amount of butter for about 10 to 15 minutes.

Doves, the Hard Way (French)

My father and brother and I sometimes used to get a small mess of birds, and my mother would do them Pyrenees Style.

Season the cleaned birds with salt and pepper, dust them with flour, and brown them thoroughly in butter. Put them into a heavy kettle. For about 24 birds, add 1 onion, chopped; 1 carrot, sliced; 2 stalks of celery, thinly sliced; 2 tomatoes, chopped (or a small can); a sprig of fresh marjoram (or about ¼ teaspoon crumbled dried); a sprig of fresh thyme (or about ¼ teaspoon crumbled dried); a large clove of garlic, minced or mashed; about 2 cups canned chicken broth; and about 1 cup dry red table wine. Cover tightly and simmer until you can easily pull a leg off the carcass, about 1 hour. Remove the birds and keep warm. Finish the juices in one of two ways:

1 Strain the juices, saving the vegetables. Whirl the vegetables with a small amount of the juices in a blender until smooth. Return the puréed vegetables to the juices along with the birds and heat through; correct seasonings.

2 Strain the juices and discard the vegetables. Return juices to kettle. Thicken juices slightly if they need it. (For about 3 cups juices: Stir together 4 tablespoons flour and 4 tablespoons cold water until smooth. Gradually whisk into bubbling juices. Heat and stir until juices are slightly thickened and smooth. Simmer, stirring, for about 3 more minutes.) Or you might have to add a little chicken broth if the juices have cooked down too much. But don't add any more wine.

Return doves to the sauce, heat through, and correct seasonings. Serve doves and sauce on top of Cheese Polenta (recipe page 114). Makes about 8 servings.

Pheasant Breasts, Bourbon

There are a million ways to do pheasant, but this is my pet way. Serve this with Rice Roberta (page 117) and Brussels sprouts.

Cut the breast pieces out of the bird so you have two nice boneless pieces of meat; set aside. Crush the remaining carcass. Put into a baking pan, and brown in a 500° oven. Add enough water to loosen the bones from the pan. Put the bones and water and brown drippings in the pan into a big pot with enough water to cover. Cover and simmer for 1 hour. Take out the bones. Boil the stock, uncovered, until it is reduced by about half. Meantime, season the breasts with salt and pepper and dust them with flour. In a frying pan, sauté them on both sides in a generous amount of butter just until they take on a little color on the outside and are cooked not quite through to the inside. Put them on a warm platter and into a 300° oven with the oven door open. (Don't close the oven door because you only want to keep the breasts warm— not keep cooking them.) Remove the excess butter from the frying pan. Add the reduced stock. Cook over high heat, stirring, until it is a thick bubbling thing—just a thin cloaking over the bottom of the pan. Add about 1½ ounces of bourbon and let that reduce a little bit. Then add a lot of commercial sour cream and a dash of Tabasco. Stir it to a smooth sauce, season it with a little A.1. sauce and salt and freshly ground black pepper. Add the pheasant breasts from the oven. Don't cook them much, just work them around in the sauce until heated through. Serve them immediately with the sauce over them.

Flipped Venison Steak

My wife and I have hunted in California, Nevada, Wyoming, Mexico. We end up using the meat for salami, and that is absolutely the most!

The big, thick venison steak guy is not for me, and neither is the roast or stew guy—not if you can get a piece of beef just as easily.

If you have to cook venison steak, fry it in a pan quickly. And never start with steaks over a half inch thick. Flip, bang, thank you, man. And this way venison can be tender—if you do it right.

Rabbit My Way

You can get fancy like the French recipes usually say. But that's a lot of crap. What you really want to do is to get down there and eat rabbit and have a good time doing it.

If you want to, you can have a few doves on hand, and flour and brown those and put them in—or some quail, or some pheasant.

Now with this, you use polenta. Make the polenta as on page

114, without or with the cheese. That is what you eat with this stew—that, with a lot of red wine to drink, a green salad, and nothing else. That's the way they cook rabbit up in the Pyrenees, that's how I do it—not the fancy way they do it in Paris!

Take a rabbit, the whole thing—legs, back, chest, not the fur—and cut it up. Put it into an earthenware bowl. Put in a chopped onion, a clove of garlic split, a bay leaf, some chopped celery, a few whole allspice, salt and pepper, and pour on enough red wine to cover it all. Cover it and stick it in the icebox for 24 hours. Then take the rabbit out, dry the pieces, flour them, and brown them well over medium heat in plenty of butter. Add liquid—at least 1 cup of chicken broth and 1 cup of the strained marinade. Cover and simmer. About a half hour later, add some peeled and lengthwise-sliced carrots, some peeled whole small boiling onions, a clove of garlic chopped, and a bay leaf. Add a pinch of thyme if you like it. Simmer it until everything is tender—the rabbit, the carrots, the onions. It'll take another half to three-quarters of an hour. Season to taste. And that's gonna turn into a nice dark brown wonderful stew. Makes about 4 servings.

Young Rabbit

Now if you've got a nice young rabbit, just flour it and fry it like chicken. Season it with salt and pepper. Geez, it's beautiful, very good.

Quick Game Stews

Now don't say "The guy's crazy!" until you try this. This is a new method, so don't knock it; it works. Making usual stews is generally a lot of work, and many times the meat turns out not so good.

First, you make a sauce the easy way: Take a can of brown gravy and a can of Chef Boy-ar-dee spaghetti sauce with mushrooms and add a little white wine, a dash of Tabasco, and a dash of A.1. sauce. Let it cook together for 20 minutes. You can even add a small can each of drained carrots, onions, and potatoes to the sauce (all are cooked in the can and need no additional cooking).

Now cube your meat (venison, all kinds of game, or even beef) into small pieces ¾ inch on a side, salt and pepper it, and flour it very, very lightly. Have your dinner ready to serve and your sauce hot and ready. Fry the meat *quickly* in a little butter to brown. *Do not* cook beyond the medium-rare state, or better even the rare. Drop the meat into the sauce, and serve *now*. Don't let it stand around or the meat will get tough.

BARBECUING
BIG STUFF, LITTLE STUFF,
SHOW-OFF COOKING

Hell, I'm not a barbecue cook. I can do it. I've done it. But I'm not what you'd call a champion. I'm a frying pan and griddle cook.

But lots of guys do like to barbecue, so why not do it? Some pretty good stuff can come from a barbecue fire. Some lousy stuff, too.

But there are a few things I can tell you about barbecuing.

At the first of the book, I tell you how you can tell when a steak is done when you're panbroiling or doing it on a griddle. The same rules still hold true if you're doing your steak over hot coals on a barbecue grill. Just follow the same ways to test for raw, rare, medium, and so forth.

Now lots of guys are keen on barbecuing chicken breasts or duck breasts with the bone in. And you see it coming, and you think, goddammit, I've got to go through this again—especially the ladies think that. That's hard to eat.

Now I don't do that. If I've got some wild ducks, I cut out the breast, and then I've got tender little pieces of meat. I dip those in soy, barbecue them over hot coals for three to five minutes on each side, and serve them rare. If you do that, you've got the very best duck you've ever had in your life. You've got to experiment with this a little to get your coals and your timing just right. I can't tell you what you've got to learn by experience.

You can do the same thing with chicken breasts.

You can do shrimp this way: Split big shelled or unshelled shrimp or prawns in half, butterfly fashion. Flavor them with any kind of flavoring crap you've got around—salt, pepper, garlic, a touch of thyme. Put them in a buttered hinged wire broiler, and slowly grill over low coals, basting with butter, just until they turn pink and lose translucency.

Trout is fabulous done over barbecue coals. But don't use a hot fire with fish. For trout—or for any fish—use a hinged wire broiler. Butter the trout well, season it with salt and pepper, and clamp it inside a buttered hinged broiler. Put it over nice coals, not too hot. With this hinged broiler, you can turn the fish over easy; you don't have to worry about it sticking to the grill. Always use a hinged broiler for small fish.

Here's an idea when you're barbecuing trout or salmon or beef. If you can, get some green oak leaves or twigs. Put a few of them onto your hot coals, and that'll make smoke. A little smoke will make your fish or steak taste good.

Vegetable thoughts with barbecuing. There are a couple of things you can do that will make anything you barbecue taste good—lamb or beef or chicken or fish or pork or whatever. One is fried bananas and fried pineapple spears and fried green papaya slices. Just slice 'em and fry them in butter in a frying pan. You may think I'm all wet. But you try this and then write me and tell me what you think, because I know this is good. Another is the recipe on page 79 for Fried Peppered Cabbage. You say aaah, aaah, who wants cabbage? Well, not aaah, aaah. You make this to go with your barbecued meats and your guests are gonna love you till hell freezes over.

About woods for barbecuing. Any resinous woods such as pine and cedar: don't use 'em—no way! I wouldn't use redwood either. You can use birch. You can use cottonwood if you can get the fire going. You can use aspen, oak, hickory, any of the close-grained, nonresinous woods. But really steer clear of any of the pines or cedars. They're no good.

There are a lot of pros and cons to the idea of using eucalyptus for smoke barbecuing. But I think it is fantastic. I've barbecued with eucalyptus wood and had a helluva nice result—to my taste. What you do is build your fire with regular wood. On the edge, put a few green leaves or twigs of eucalyptus. So you use oak or other good wood for the fire, but use the eucalyptus for the smoke flavor. It's terrific.

To get a charcoal fire started: If you don't have an electric starter, you can use bourbon or gin or some other alcohol. Jeezus, the way they're thinning down the bourbon and gin these days, I doubt if you can light anything with it until you get it a little hot. Rubbing alcohol is the best thing, or a can of Sterno is good.

These inflammable liquid and jelly charcoal lighter fluids don't warn you of this on their labels. But if you're going to use that stuff, be damn sure that you get all of your charcoal burning all over so you can eliminate all the fumes from the lighter fluid. A lot of times guys get the center of their fire burning and still have their periphery coals covered with unburned lighter fluid when they start to cook. It makes the result smell and taste awful.

If you barbecue with charcoal and want some smoke: Get hardwood sawdust and wet it or go out to the country and get some twigs, and put these along the edge of your barbecue fire; you can make all the smoke you want with either of these. Very simple.

Barbecued Whole Lamb

This happened a thousand years ago. I barbecued a lamb, a whole damn carcass.

I tied the animal on a spit with a crank on it, put it over a slow fire, and turned it. I made a sauce of a quart of prepared mustard, some catsup, chopped garlic, oil, red wine vinegar, a bottle of Worcestershire sauce, and 2 or 3 tablespoons sugar, some pepper, and some chopped celery. This sounds crazy as hell. It was crazy as hell. Before I started cooking, I had the lamb nice and dry. I splashed on some sauce all over the outside and let it dry a little. Then I slowly started to cook it. How long? That depends on your meat and your fire. I cooked it till it was done. All the time it was cooking, I kept sloshing the sauce on with a big paintbrush. See, the idea here is not to cook all the juice out of the meat before you've cooked the meat. If you cook slowly to get a crust on the outside, then you'll seal the juices in. When it came time to serve, I put a bowl of the barbecue sauce on the table, so people could dip the cooked meat into it if they wanted to. Well, this was fabulous.

Mai Tai Kebab, Bob Bercu, Honolulu

⅓ cup soy sauce	Whole mushrooms
⅓ cup salad oil	Cherry tomatoes
⅓ cup good dry red wine	Green bell peppers, cut into
1½ pounds beef sirloin or filet,	1-inch squares
cut into 1- to 1½-inch cubes	Small boiling onions, peeled

Mix together soy sauce, oil, and wine. Pour over beef, and turn to mix well. Cover and allow to marinate, chilled, for at least 6 hours. Thread beef onto skewers, alternating with vegetables. Broil over hot coals, basting frequently with remaining marinade, until meat is done to your preference.

Sam Morse's Steaks with Mustard Sauce

This is Sam's recipe just as he gave it to me:

I don't know any better way to cook steaks than to get a good bit of charcoal good and hot, put the steaks on the fire, let them burn a little on the outside, and when they look just right, take them off. I have a way of sort of bouncing my tongs on a steak as it is cooking. When the steak bounces, it is usually done. A good thick sirloin usually takes about fifteen minutes to cook. It is a little charred on the outside and still red on the inside.

I find the only successful way to make mustard sauce is right on top of the steaks. I take a big, specially made pan that I have, which reaches across my grill so that I can get it warm. I put the cooked steaks in this pan with plenty of pepper and salt on them to start with, cut a few of them in half so that they will bleed, and spread a layer of dry mustard on each one of the steaks. Then I use a generous amount of butter, which I have allowed to soften in the sun or at the side of the fire, and sprinkle on quite a bit of Worcestershire sauce. I then turn the steaks over and swish them around until the sauce is smooth.

So far, with several thousands of steaks, I have never had a complaint. There is one thing that is essential—you have to have good meat to start with.

About Some Little Things Called Eggs

Now those nice little hens didn't put a cute little shell around those eggs to protect them from your beating their brains out in cooking. You know, eggs are tender little things. So handle them with care—in making an omelet or anything else. Don't go cooking the hell out of 'em. Eggs can taste pretty lousy if they are cooked till hell won't have 'em. Take it easy, fellows.

Hawaiian Ham and Eggs

I've put this recipe into every cookbook I've written, I guess; it's such a great dish! Here is the story.

My dad was an old French-Canadian and a helluva cook. On Sunday mornings before he opened his little grocery store, he'd make breakfast for us—my mom, my brother, and me. Sometimes it'd be fried bananas and pineapple with ham and eggs.

Here's how he'd do it for each serving. He'd start with a heavy skillet and medium heat. First, he'd fry a slice of canned pineapple in a little butter, and take it out and put in on a warm platter. Then he'd split a banana lengthwise, and he'd fry that in the same pan with lots more butter. That made juice, and the pineapple had made juice. So he'd fry the banana pretty thoroughly until nicely browned, and then flip it out smoothly onto the platter. Then he'd add more butter, and fry a thick center ham slice in that and then put the ham on the platter. When he had the ham fried, there was a lot more juice in the pan, and then he'd add more butter. Then he'd put the eggs in there to fry, and it was just like poaching eggs in butter and juice. Season them with salt and pepper if you need to, and put them on the platter. That's the best ham and eggs I've ever tasted.

Crab Chawan Mushi

This can be a first course, or a supper when you're sick.

Don't try to hold this before serving. Serve it the minute it's done. Otherwise it will begin to weep.

4 eggs

About 4 cups mildly seasoned chicken broth, fat removed

1 teaspoon sweet sake or sherry

½ teaspoon soy sauce

⅛ teaspoon salt

⅛ teaspoon monosodium glutamate

1/16 teaspoon sugar

12 1-inch sprigs watercress

8 thin strips fresh lemon peel (outer yellow part only)

4 small cooked and shelled crab legs

6 tablespoons flaked cooked crab meat

Beat eggs lightly, just until whites and yolks are thoroughly blended. Measure beaten eggs, and add 4 times their quantity of broth. Add sake, soy sauce, salt, monosodium glutamate, and sugar and mix well. Divide watercress, lemon peel, and crab among 4 custard or soup cups (each about 1¼-cup size). Pour egg mixture into cups. Cover each with foil or loosely with its own lid. Place on a rack in a large kettle above gently boiling water. Cover kettle and steam custards for 20 minutes or until slender knife inserted near center comes out clean (cut through foil). Serve immediately. Makes 4 servings.

Basic Omelet

Beat 3 eggs, 1 tablespoon water, and ⅛ teaspoon salt vigorously with a fork until blended. Melt 1 tablespoon butter in an 8-inch omelet pan over medium-high heat until it bubbles and begins to brown. Pour eggs into pan, and tilt pan so egg covers bottom. Lift egg edges with a thin-bladed spatula and tilt pan so uncooked egg flows to bottom of pan; cook until top is still creamy and not quite set. Fold top third of omelet over, and slip out of pan onto warm serving plate, rolling pan so that folded section falls over its extended edge. Makes 1 serving.

Pistachio Omelet

Texture is so important in making up a good dish. You need the noise. Croutons and pistachios give it here.

Combine 1½ tablespoons grated Parmesan cheese and 2 tablespoons finely chopped fresh parsley in a paper bag. Add croutons (recipe below) and shake to coat. Make a moist basic 3-egg omelet according to recipe above *except:* Before folding, sprinkle croutons down center. Top with about 2 tablespoons coarsely chopped pistachios. Fold omelet and slip out of pan onto warm serving plate. Sprinkle with a *few* more chopped pistachios and the cheese and parsley remaining in bag. Makes 1 serving.

Croutons   Trim crusts off French bread (preferably sour dough) slices, and cut into ½ inch cubes; measure ¾ cup. In a frying pan, sauté cubes in about 1½ tablespoons butter over medium heat until crisp and brown.

Crouton Omelet

Make this exactly as the pistachio omelet above *except* omit the pistachios, add ⅛ teaspoon crushed dried red peppers to the Parmesan mixture, and increase the parsley to 3 tablespoons. If you want to, top the omelet with a little nice Cheddar cheese sauce before you sprinkle it with the final crumbs.

Hayden Head's Salmon Omelet, Corpus Christi Style

We often go down to Texas in the fall for dove and quail shooting. Hayden Head and his bride, Annie Blake, have a parcel of ground down around Crystal City. Hayden loves to cook, and his specialty is this omelet. It's absolutely crazy and it's good. What a thing this is if you can get the right hot Texas relish. The relish is the important thing, but you can fudge it with a good India relish and liberal use of something else hot.

1 medium-sized onion, finely chopped
6 tablespoons butter
1 large ripe tomato, peeled, seeded, and chopped
1½ tablespoons Texas sweet-hot relish, or 2 teaspoons sweet India relish mixed with 2 teaspoons minced canned jalapeño peppers, or 1 tablespoon sweet India relish mixed with ¼ teaspoon crumbled dried hot red peppers or 4 generous dashes Tabasco

8 eggs
2 tablespoons cream or milk
Salt and freshly ground black pepper
1 can (7½ ounces) salmon, drained, skin and large bones removed, and salmon broken into large pieces

In a large frying pan over medium heat, sauté onions in butter until limp. Stir in tomato and relish. Beat eggs with cream and with salt and pepper to season. Add to frying pan and softly scramble just until set, adding the salmon near the end of the scrambling so it just heats through. Serve immediately. Makes 4 servings.

Zucchini Omelet

When you do this right, the zucchini tastes like oysters. Be sure to choose young, tender, small zucchini. And fry thin slices *quickly* in butter; they *must* be brown and almost crisp. This is fabulous.

Trim ends from about ¼-pound young, small zucchini. Slice zucchini ⅛ inch thick or less. In a heavy frying pan over high heat, sauté zucchini in about 1½ tablespoons butter until brown.

Season with salt and pepper. Add about 1 teaspoon dehydrated minced onions which have been soaked in water until moist and drained. Make a moist basic 3-egg omelet according to recipe page 75 *except:* Before folding, turn zucchini down center. Fold omelet and slip out of pan onto warm serving plate. Makes 1 serving.

Chinese Hamburger Omelet

This is really a scrambled egg dish made into a flat patty or cake about a half inch thick like Foo Yung. My Chinese cook does this for me at home, and I like it very much. It is so easy to cook. Serve a green salad with it.

In a heavy frying pan about 8 inches in diameter over high heat, cook about 2 ounces ground round in 1 tablespoon butter until meat is brown and a little crisp. Add 2 tablespoons very finely chopped onions, and sauté until limp. Reduce heat to medium. Season meat with salt and generously with freshly ground black pepper. Melt 1 tablespoon more butter in bottom of pan. Beat 3 eggs, pour evenly over meat, and gently lift eggs around edges to let uncooked portions flow to bottom of pan. When eggs are set, gently loosen all over bottom with a flexible spatula, and gently slip the mixture out, flat, onto a warm serving plate. Sprinkle generously with finely chopped fresh parsley. Makes 1 serving.

Sweetbread Omelet

If you want to make a festive lunch, try this.

For each serving you'll need ¼ pound of sweetbreads prepared Trader Vic Style (recipe page 18) *except* cut sweetbreads into ½-inch pieces, and ¼ cup croutons (recipe page 75—with Pistachio Omelet). Make a sloppy 3-egg omelet (recipe page 75), but before you fold it, spoon your sweetbreads down the center, and top them with croutons. Fold the omelet over and roll it out onto a plate for a really fat-looking omelet. Sprinkle it with finely chopped fresh parsley. If you follow this formula and you still don't like the way it tastes, let me know. I'd like to hear about it because this is a damn good thing to eat.

About Some Lousy Things Called VEGETABLES

If you don't eat vegetables, you'll die. So you might as well cook 'em so they taste good and then enjoy them.

Fried Peppered Cabbage

This is the best vegetable you ever ate in your ever-lovin' life, because it is just great with all kinds of meats from steaks to sausages—instead of spinach or peas. I think I like it best with blood sausage which has been slowly browned in butter. This doesn't taste like cabbage.

1 medium-sized head white cabbage
¼ cup butter
Salt and freshly ground black pepper
3 tablespoons commercial sour cream

Wash cabbage, remove core, and cut cabbage into ¼-inch squares. Melt butter in a large frying pan over high heat. Add cabbage, and sauté, turning constantly, for about 1 minute, just until cabbage is tender-crisp (it should not wilt or cook through). Season with salt and very generously with pepper. Stir in sour cream. Makes about 6 servings.

Broccoli Puffs

Vegetables are usually boring. Jeezus, they don't even look like much on your plate. So let's make 'em look appealing and make them into little puddings. I call them puffs. You can make them of any lightly cooked, chopped vegetable—broccoli, string beans, peas, spinach.

Just follow this recipe and substitute whatever vegetable you want for the broccoli. If you're using green beans, add a half teaspoon of crushed dried basil.

3 tablespoons minced green onions with part of green tops
1 tablespoon butter
3 eggs
1 cup heavy (whipping) cream
About ½ teaspoon salt
About ⅛ teaspoon freshly ground black pepper
½ teaspoon ground nutmeg
Dash of Tabasco
1 tablespoon minced fresh parsley
2 cups finely chopped cooked fresh broccoli
About 3 tablespoons grated Parmesan cheese

Sauté onions in butter until limp. Beat eggs and beat in cream, salt, pepper, nutmeg, and Tabasco. Add onions, parsley, and broccoli, and mix well. Pour into 4 or 6 small buttered ramekins. Sprinkle with Parmesan. Bake in a 350° oven until golden and puffed and knife inserted in center comes out clean, about 20 to 25 minutes. Makes 4 or 6 servings.

Asparagus, Chinese Style

This makes asparagus taste like asparagus doesn't taste. You don't boil the asparagus, you fry it. It turns out crisp and flavorful, and it's a whole new flavor. You serve it like a vegetable on your plate alongside meat.

Use green asparagus, not white.

2 pounds fresh asparagus
2 tablespoons salad oil
3 ounces ground or minced lean
   pork
½ teaspoon salt
⅛ teaspoon sugar

¼ cup chicken broth
1 teaspoon cornstarch mixed
   with 2 teaspoons cold water
   and 1 teaspoon Kikkoman soy
   sauce

Snap off tough ends of asparagus. Slice asparagus sharply on the diagonal into 1-inch lengths. Heat salad oil over medium-high to high heat in a wide, heavy frying pan or wok until it ripples when pan is tipped. Add pork and quickly stir for about 30 seconds. Add asparagus and turn in pork and oil. Add salt, sugar, and broth. Cover and cook, turning once or twice, just until asparagus steams through and is very crisp and barely tender, about 2 minutes for thin spears. Uncover, sprinkle with cornstarch mixture, and turn just until cornstarch mixture clears and barely binds asparagus. Makes 4 generous servings.

Carrots Niu

You have to have thick coconut milk to make this recipe. Try to buy canned frozen unsweetened coconut milk and thaw it. If you can't buy thick coconut milk, you can make your own from a fresh coconut: Pour ¾ cup boiling water over the grated meat of 1 coconut (to grate fresh shelled and peeled ripe coconut easily: whirl small pieces in a blender). Stir coconut and press down with a spoon. Allow to stand for 20 minutes. Turn coconut into several thicknesses of cheesecloth to strain; squeeze to extract all liquid. If necessary in order to make 1 cup liquid, add a little more water.

1 tablespoon dehydrated minced
   onions soaked in water until
   moist and drained, or 2
   tablespoons minced fresh
   green onions
4 tablespoons butter
8 carrots, peeled and cut into
   ½-inch diagonal slices
⅓ cup thick coconut milk

2 tablespoons dry white table
   wine
2 tablespoons chicken broth
1 teaspoon raw or brown sugar
About ½ teaspoon salt
About ⅛ teaspoon freshly
   ground black pepper
Finely chopped fresh parsley

In a large frying pan, sauté onions in butter until soft. Stir in carrots. Add coconut milk, wine, broth, sugar, and salt and pepper to season. Cover and cook over medium heat until carrots are tender but firm, about 15 minutes. Sprinkle with parsley. Makes 3 to 4 servings.

Chinese Kraut

Not too long ago when I asked Ah Lo, my Chinese cook at home, what he was serving for dinner, he told me sauerkraut cooked Chinese style. Chinese sauerkraut??? Ah Lo told me that the Chinese have made sauerkraut since they built the Great Wall in China, and that Marco Polo brought sauerkraut back to the Western world.

If you want to make this into a main dish, add some pork chops: brown the chops, season with salt and pepper, and arrange them in a single layer in a baking pan with the sauerkraut layered above and below them. Cover and bake in a 350° oven for 45 minutes or until tender. Add a little more broth if necessary to keep it moist during baking. Or add bratwurst: slowly brown the sausages in butter, and then bake with the sauerkraut as above for about 20 minutes.

1 large can (1 pound 11 ounces) sauerkraut	2 tablespoons salad oil
Cold water	1 tablespoon firmly packed brown sugar
1 medium-sized onion, finely chopped	Salt and freshly ground black pepper
1 medium-sized ripe tomato, peeled, seeded, and chopped	1 cup chicken broth

Drain sauerkraut, cover with cold water, and let stand for about 15 minutes. Rinse well in cold running water and drain. In a large frying pan, sauté sauerkraut, onion, and tomato in salad oil, stirring, until onions are limp. Stir in sugar, about ¼ teaspoon pepper, and broth. Simmer, uncovered, for 25 minutes or until liquid disappears; stir occasionally. Correct seasoning with salt and pepper. Makes 5 to 6 servings.

Spinach Potato Pancakes

Potatoes are goddam things, hard to eat sometimes. Potatoes—a-a-a-ch! But here's a way to make 'em taste good—in pancakes with spinach. You fry these little children all crisp on the outside, and here you've got a nice way to take on potatoes.

If you need to, you can make these a little while ahead and hold them in a warm oven or reheat them in a hot oven for serving.

1 large raw potato (10 ounces), peeled
2 eggs, separated
1½ tablespoons minced fresh onions
1 package (10 or 12 ounces) frozen chopped spinach, thawed, drained, and excess water pressed out

About ½ teaspoon salt
About ¼ teaspoon freshly ground black pepper
Butter

Coarsely shred potato into strips (as for hashed brown potatoes). Place in a sieve for about 15 minutes to allow excess moisture to drain off. Beat egg yolks slightly; mix with onions, spinach, potato, salt, and pepper. Beat egg whites until stiff but not dry, and fold in. Melt a generous amount of butter in a heavy frying pan or on a griddle over medium heat until it bubbles. For each pancake, spoon one-eighth of the mixture into pan, shaping a 3- to 4-inch circle. Cook until crisp and brown on one side, lift, add more butter to pan if necessary, turn, and brown on second side. Makes 8 pancakes.

Chinese-fried Zucchini

Get small zucchini. Don't peel 'em, but brush the hairy stuff off the outside and wash and dry them. Slice them thinly. Then toss them in a generous amount of butter in a heavy frying pan over high heat for a couple of minutes. Add a little chicken broth and salt to season. Put the lid on and steam them for a minute or two, and serve. They come out pretty raw. But they're damn good to eat.

Nutmeg Spinach

2 tablespoons dehydrated
  minced onions, soaked in
  water until moist and drained
6 tablespoons butter
2 packages (10 ounces each)
  frozen chopped spinach,
  thawed

½ teaspoon ground nutmeg
Pinch of sugar
Salt and freshly ground black
  pepper

In a large frying pan, sauté onions in butter until tender. Stir in spinach, cover, and cook over medium heat until spinach is heated through and tender, about 8 minutes. Stir in nutmeg, sugar, salt, and pepper. Makes 6 servings.

MUSHROOMS

Well, fellas, this isn't the only cookbook you've got. I like mushrooms. You fry them or you put 'em in a sauce. And I don't want to write about mushrooms. Look 'em up in another book.

Beans My Mother's Style

Sundays, we used to have a roasted leg of lamb. Monday we'd have sliced leg of lamb heated over in gravy. Tuesday we had lamb patties. And Wednesday we had navy white beans cooked with the lamb bone left over from the roast leg. So here's how you do it. It's a lot like My Cassoulet, page 122. But here you've got one helluva nice dinner just with beans.

1 leg of lamb bone left over
  from a roast
1 pound dry small white (navy)
  beans, rinsed
Water
2 medium-sized onions, finely
  chopped
1 large can (1 pound 12 ounces)
  tomatoes, broken up

2 large cloves garlic, minced or
  mashed
1 large bay leaf
Freshly ground black pepper
Salt
2 tablespoons dry white table
  wine
2 tablespoons finely chopped
  fresh parsley

Put the bone and the beans into a large kettle. Add about 5 cups cold water. Cover and heat to boiling, boil for 2 minutes, remove from heat, and let stand for 1 hour. Stir in onions, tomatoes, garlic, bay leaf, and about ½ teaspoon pepper. Heat to boiling, then cover and simmer until beans are tender, about 1½ to 2 hours. (Add a little more water if you need to in order to keep the beans a little soupy.) Add salt to taste and more pepper if you like. Stir in wine. Sprinkle with parsley. Makes about 6 main-dish or 8 vegetable servings.

ARTICHOKES

Most people eat artichokes one leaf at a time, and then sometimes they take two leaves, and then sometimes they just cook the artichoke bottoms and eat that. This is a vegetable you can do a lot with.

One of the best things is to slice the cooked bottoms and fry them in butter simply with a few shallots and some parsley. A recipe follows. Or go to a delicatessen or fancy food store and get a can of chanterelle mushrooms, slice them, and fry them along with the artichoke slices.

And then you can leave the artichoke bottoms whole. And you can stuff their little bottoms with a whole bunch of stuff. Here are a couple of ideas of what you can stuff 'em with.

Artichoke Bottoms Tahitian

Rinse large canned artichoke bottoms well. Place in simmering water until heated through. Drain well. Fill cavity of each generously with Tahitian green beans (recipe below). Sprinkle with minced fresh parsley.

Tahitian green beans   Sauté 2 tablespoons minced green onions with part of green tops in ⅓ cup butter until limp. Add 1 cup of 1-inch lengths of French-cut green beans which have been cooked just until tender-crisp; 1 tablespoon peeled, seeded, and diced fresh ripe tomatoes; ⅛ teaspoon crumbled dried sweet basil, and a pinch of sugar. Toss to heat through and mix. Season well with salt and freshly ground black pepper.

Glazed Artichoke Bottoms

You can buy a good brand of frozen creamed spinach and season it up with nutmeg, and you won't have to go through the whole rigmarole of making creamed spinach yourself. Or you can make your own creamed spinach.

Rinse large canned artichoke bottoms well. Place in simmering water until heated through. Drain well. Heap each bottom full of hot creamed spinach seasoned with nutmeg. Put a generous spoonful of Hollandaise Sauce (recipe page 44) over the top. Broil about 6 inches from heat until Hollandaise glazes to a light brown.

GREEN BEANS

Jeezus. Shirley Sarvis is helping me write this book, and she said to me, "Now what about a green bean recipe?" And I said, "I hate green beans." "All right," she said, "let's leave them out." I say, "No, some silly bastard will like green beans."

The first thing to do is to find out something about the green beans you're cooking. The long, long Chinese beans are the best. Or get the long stringless kind. Whatever you do, try to get fresh green beans.

Macadamia Buttered Beans

About 1 pound fresh green beans
½ cup butter
1½ tablespoons fresh lemon juice
Generous grinding of black pepper
½ cup chopped salted and roasted macadamia nuts

Trim and French-cut beans, and cook in boiling salted water until barely tender; drain. Meantime, in a small pan, heat butter until it foams, then browns lightly. Stir in lemon juice, pepper, and nuts. Pour over hot beans. Makes 4 vegetable servings.

Pine Nut Buttered Beans

1 pound fresh green beans
½ cup butter
½ cup lightly toasted pine nuts
¼ teaspoon salt
Generous grinding of black
pepper

¼ teaspoon crumbled dried
sweet basil
1½ tablespoons minced fresh
parsley
1 teaspoon fresh lemon juice

Trim and French-cut beans, and cook in boiling salted water until barely tender; drain. Meantime, in a small pan over medium heat, melt butter until it begins to foam; do not brown. Stir in nuts, salt, pepper, basil, parsley, and lemon juice. Pour over hot beans. Makes 4 servings.

Pistachio Buttered Beans

1 pound fresh green beans
½ cup butter
½ cup lightly toasted chopped
pistachio nuts
¼ teaspoon salt

Generous grinding of black
pepper
2 teaspoons minced fresh
parsley
1 teaspoon fresh lemon juice

Trim and French-cut beans, and cook in boiling salted water until barely tender; drain. Meantime, in a small pan over medium heat, melt butter until it begins to foam; do not brown. Stir in nuts, salt, pepper, parsley, and lemon juice. Pour over hot beans. Makes 4 servings.

SALADS WITH THINGS AND STUFF

I don't know why, but more people get a gastronomical hotfoot making a salad. They think that the thing is going to blow up or taste like the inside of a motorman's glove or a Greek wrestler's hatband.

But a salad is really a simple and wonderful thing to do. You don't need to get in a great big tizz to make a salad. It's easy. Most things are on the supermarket shelf or in the refrigerator. You can do wonderful things with simple ideas like using half sour cream and half mayonnaise for a dressing.

And now remember this, fellas. Calories do count, especially in some of these old-fashioned dressings like olive oil or mayonnaise. That stuff's old hat.

Olive oil never helped anybody's salad. I don't care who they are. It's a heavy, lousy, greasy, stinking oil. It'll kill you. Safflower oil and corn oil are wonderful oils.

Make your mayonnaise with safflower or corn oil. Even then, your mayonnaise will be pretty rich. So you can lighten it up with a little sour cream. Then you've got a good dressing. It wraps itself around whatever you're doing with it.

Trader Vic's Mayonnaise

There are guys who like to cook who are a little too much of purists. But there's one thing I'm a purist about, and that's mayonnaise. Geeze, if you want a mayonnaise that will make your salads taste really good, make it out of red wine vinegar and good oil.

Vinegars vary in tartness, and so do people's tastes. So add the vinegar to taste.

2 egg yolks	About 1 teaspoon salt
1 teaspoon dry mustard	Freshly ground black pepper
About 2 cups safflower oil	Red wine vinegar

Put egg yolks and mustard into a bowl and beat with a wire whisk to blend thoroughly. Drip in the oil a few drops at a time, whisking vigorously. Continue dripping in the oil very gradually and whisking until the emulsion takes hold, then you can add the oil a little more generously each time you pour. If the mixture gets too thick to work, add a dash of vinegar. Add no more than 2 cups oil, less if you like the consistency with less oil. Whisk in salt and freshly ground black pepper to taste. Whisk in enough vinegar to give the degree of tartness you wish, usually about 2 tablespoons. Makes about 2 cups.

Red Wine Blender Mayonnaise

If you've got a blender, you can make a good mayonnaise faster this way.

1 egg	1 teaspoon Dijon-style mustard
1 cup safflower oil	⅜ teaspoon salt
1 tablespoon red wine vinegar	Generous grinding of black
1 tablespoon fresh lemon juice	pepper

Place egg, ¼ cup of the oil, the vinegar, lemon juice, mustard, salt, and pepper in blender container. Whirl at high speed until smooth. Remove blender top and slowly pour in remaining oil, continuing to whirl the mixture until smooth and thick. Makes about 1 cup.

Oh-So-Good Peachy Salad Dressing

This is great on a salad of crab or shrimp and salad greens, or just on mixed salad greens. I used to sometimes put a little A.1. sauce in this, too.

1½ cups safflower oil
9 tablespoons fresh lemon juice
2 tablespoons red wine vinegar
1 tablespoon Dijon-style mustard
1¼ teaspoons salt
About ¼ teaspoon freshly ground black pepper
About ½ teaspoon concentrated beef extract (such as Bovril)
3 tablespoons finely chopped fresh parsley
2 tablespoons minced green onions with part of green tops

Shake or beat all ingredients together thoroughly. Makes about 2 cups.

Wasabi Dressing

Maybe two or three of you guys know what wasabi powder is, but I'll bet most of you never heard of the stuff. It is Japanese horseradish in powdered form. You get it in cans in Oriental markets. First before you use it, you have to reconstitute it with a little water to make a paste.

Here is a new dressing, Wasabi Dressing. You use it just the way it is on everything from chilled, poached fish and mixed green salads to cold seafood cocktails and grated celery root. Use it or Wasabi-Watercress Dressing where you want to have a pungent good dressing.

If you can't get wasabi, make a similar dressing with Dijon-style mustard (recipe below).

To reconstitute wasabi for use: Mix the powder with cold water until it is of mayonnaise consistency; cover and let stand for 5 minutes to allow flavors to develop.

¼ cup wasabi powder, reconstituted
¾ cup commercial sour cream
¾ cup mayonnaise
1 tablespoon fresh lemon juice
1½ teaspoons red wine vinegar
½ teaspoon sugar
Salt and freshly ground black pepper

Stir together all ingredients. Makes about 1½ cups dressing.

Wasabi-Watercress Dressing

Fold 1 cup finely chopped watercress sprigs into Wasabi Dressing (above).

Mustard Dressing

¾ cup commercial sour cream
¾ cup mayonnaise
1½ to 2 tablespoons Dijon-style
  mustard
1 tablespoon fresh lemon juice

1½ teaspoons red wine vinegar
½ teaspoon sugar
Salt and freshly ground black
  pepper

Stir together all ingredients. Makes about 1½ cups dressing.

Mustard-Watercress Dressing

Fold 1 cup finely chopped watercress sprigs into Mustard Dressing (above).

Sauerkraut and Garbanzo Bean Salad

Fella, sometime you want to cook something that's crazy. Well, sauerkraut and garbanzo bean salad is crazy as hell—but good crazy.

1 large can (1 pound
  11 ounces) sauerkraut
1 can (15 ounces) garbanzo
  beans, drained
About ⅓ cup snipped fresh
  chives
Trader Vic's mustard dressing
  (recipe below)

Salt and freshly ground black
  pepper
Crisp lettuce leaves
4 ounces cooked smoked
  German salami such as
  Thuringer or Mettwurst, cut
  into julienne strips
Pepper cress or watercress

Thoroughly rinse sauerkraut with cold water. Place in a kettle with cold water to cover, heat to boiling, and simmer, uncovered, for 10 minutes. Drain well and chill. Combine sauerkraut, beans, and chives in a salad bowl. Mix thoroughly with enough dressing to moisten. Add salt and pepper to season well. Arrange each salad on a lettuce-lined chilled plate. Sprinkle with salami. Top with pepper cress or watercress sprigs. Makes 6 servings.

Trader Vic's mustard dressing   Beat together thoroughly with a fork 4 tablespoons mayonnaise, 3 tablespoons salad oil, 1 tablespoon white wine vinegar, 1 tablespoon Dijon-style mustard, 2 teaspoons fresh lemon juice, ¼ teaspoon salt, and ⅛ teaspoon pepper.

Watercress and Endive Salad

4 heads Belgian endive
8 cups watercress sprigs (loosely pack to measure)
Trader Vic's mustard dressing (recipe above)

Cut endive in half lengthwise, then thinly slice crosswise. Toss with watercress and just enough dressing to moisten well. Makes 6 salad servings.

Man's Way to Serve Belgian Endive

You don't pull it all apart. You quarter it and you lay it on a salad plate and you pour a good French dressing over it and you pick it up with your fingers and you eat it. It's damn good. Simple, too. If you want to: grind on some black pepper and add some watercress sprigs.

French Dressing

It's not a French dressing if you make it with cider vinegar. Use red wine vinegar. Now some red wine vinegars are as strong as hell. Get a good one that is not strong and mix it up to taste with oil, salt, and pepper. If you want to be fancy, you can add a *little* monosodium glutamate—not too much!—and just a *little* sugar. Anything else is not French dressing. And I still think that olive oil is lousy for a salad dressing; it makes things too greasy. Use safflower or corn or peanut oil and you'll get a good emulsion and a good dressing.

Sweetbread Salad

You can make a salad out of damn near anything. Lentil beans make a helluva salad. You can make a smoked ox tongue salad.

Well, you get ahold of some sweetbreads and boil and clean 'em and put them in a salad—just crumpled up—and see what happens.

Prepared Sweetbreads (recipe page 19), chilled

⅔ cup finely diced celery
⅓ cup minced green onions (white part only) or white onions
½ cup French Dressing (recipe page 93)

Salt and freshly ground black peper
Fresh lemon juice
Crisp lettuce
Tomato wedges and watercress sprigs for garnish

Cut or break sweetbreads into ½-inch pieces. Toss sweetbreads, celery, and onions with enough French dressing to moisten well. Season to taste with plenty of salt, pepper, and lemon juice. Arrange each salad on a lettuce-lined chilled plate. Garnish with tomato wedges and watercress sprigs. Makes 4 to 6 servings.

Lentil Salad

I got to talking to Shirley Sarvis as I was working on this book—in fact she does the legwork and I do the talking. I said, "D'you know what would make a helluva salad? Lentils. But in a special way." Now sometime when you have a bunch of people coming, make a lentil salad in a ring mold this way. Your guests will say, "Where the hell did you find this out?" It should be pretty, too.

1 cup lentils, well rinsed
1 onion stuck with 2 whole cloves
1 bay leaf
Salt
Water
1 envelope (1 tablespoon) unflavored gelatin
1 can (10½ ounces) condensed beef consommé, undiluted
1 teaspoon fresh lemon juice

Generous dash of Tabasco
3 tablespoons finely minced white onions
1 cup very finely diced celery
⅔ cup julienne strips of corned tongue
⅔ cup julienne strips of well-smoked cooked ham
Watercress sprigs
Wasabi-Watercress Dressing (recipe page 92)

Put lentils in a saucepan with onion and cloves, bay leaf, 1 teaspoon salt, and 3 cups cold water. Heat to boiling, then cover and simmer until lentils are just tender, about 30 minutes. Rinse well in cold running water and drain. Discard onion and bay leaf. Put 1¼ cups water into a saucepan. Sprinkle gelatin over top and allow to soften. Add consommé and ½ teaspoon salt; stir over low heat until gelatin is dissolved. Add lemon juice and Tabasco. Turn into a bowl and chill until syrupy. Fold in lentils, onion, celery, tongue, and ham. Pour into a 6-cup ring mold and chill until set. At serving time, unmold onto a chilled platter. Garnish with watercress. Serve with Wasabi-Watercress Dressing. Makes 6 to 8 servings.

Marinated Lentil Salad

Use the same ingredients as above *except* leave out the gelatin and consommé and watercress and Wasabi-Watercress Dressing. Cook up your beans, drain them, combine with onions, celery, tongue, and ham; and dress with half French Dressing (recipe page 93) and half Oh-So-Good Peachy Salad Dressing (page 91). Chill for a little while before serving.

Sunflower Bean Sprout Salad

6 tablespoons shelled raw
   sunflower seeds
2 pounds fresh bean sprouts
1½ cups julienne strips cooked
   chicken breast (about 1½
   whole frying chicken breasts,
   poached)
1½ cups julienne strips Chinese
   barbecued pork (cha siew,
   chahr siu) or well-smoked
   ham (about ½ pound)
1½ cups julienne strips green
   onions with part of green
   tops

1 large canned jalapeño pepper,
   seeded and very thinly sliced
Dressing (recipe below)
Salt and freshly ground black
   pepper
Crisp lettuce
Watercress sprigs, tomato
   wedges, hard-cooked egg
   slices, and black olives for
   garnish

Cover sunflower seeds with water, heat to boiling, simmer for 10 minutes, drain well, and cool. Drop sprouts into boiling water and heat until water returns to boiling, rinse in cold running water, drain well, and chill. Combine in a bowl the seeds, sprouts, chicken, pork, onions, and jalapeño. Prepare dressing. Toss salad thoroughly with enough dressing to moisten well. Correct seasoning with salt and pepper. Lift salad onto 6 lettuce-lined chilled plates. Garnish with watercress, tomatoes, egg slices, and olives. Pass additional dressing. Makes 6 luncheon salads.

Dressing Shake or beat together 1½ cups safflower oil, 9 tablespoons fresh lemon juice, 2 tablespoons red wine vinegar, 1 tablespoon Dijon-style mustard, about 1 teaspoon salt, and about ¼ teaspoon freshly ground black pepper.

Mexican Jícama Salad

I copied this straight out of my own Mexican book. I don't mind repeating when something's this good and unusual.

The *jícama* (pronounced hǐ'cama, as in hiccup) is a bulb-shaped Mexican root vegetable, although it is eaten raw as a fruit and usually mixed with fruits and vegetables in salads. Underneath its tough brown skin, the white flesh is firm, crisp, and wonderfully juicy with a delicate flavor somewhat reminiscent of an apple. Jícamas are especially good when kept chilled in the refrigerator, and can be peeled, sliced, and eaten out of hand like raw carrots or celery.

½ cup oil and vinegar dressing (recipe below)

3 cups peeled, julienned jícama

½ cup julienned salami

½ cup julienned Swiss chesse

1 large bell pepper, cut into 6 rings

Romaine lettuce

Freshly grated Parmesan cheese

Chopped chives or parsley

Prepare dressing. Combine the strips of jícama, salami, and Swiss cheese and marinate in the dressing until serving time. When ready to serve, place a portion of the salad mixture within a green pepper ring on romaine leaves. Sprinkle with Parmesan cheese and chopped chives or parsley. Makes 6 servings.

Oil and vinegar dressing Combine 3 parts oil with 1 part vinegar or fresh lemon juice. Add salt and freshly ground pepper to taste.

Wilted Watercress

What the hell do you want with wilted watercress? For a terrific salad, that's what. This is the way you'll get the full flavor out of the watercress, and the watercress won't be too hard to get into your mouth.

Take the watercress and clean it nice and take off the tough ends of the little stems and break up the sprigs into little pieces and put them into a bowl. Then you take a little oil and a little vinegar and a little Wasabi Dressing (page 91) or Mustard Dressing (page 92) and pour them over the watercress. Then, with your wooden salad servers, beat the hell out of that watercress. Just pound it up until the poor stuff is plain tired out and wilted. Then toss it with a little more of the wasabi or mustard dressing—just to cloak it well —and serve. It looks kinda tired on your plate. But you'll have a fantastic salad.

Bengal Lobster Salad

If you don't have frozen coconut milk or fresh coconut cream for the dressing, you can skip it and just use a little more mayonnaise and sour cream.

For a handsome effect, serve this luncheon salad in large clamshells lined with spears of Belgian endive or hearts of romaine. Place each salad-filled shell in the center of a slightly scooped rimless dinner plate lined with shaved ice.

You can also make this with crab meat or tiny shrimp or a mixture of both.

¾ pound cooked lobster meat
About 2 tablespoons fresh
  lemon juice
⅔ cup finely sliced celery
½ cup thinly sliced water
  chestnuts
½ cup diced fresh pineapple
6 tablespoons mango chutney,
  chopped
4 tablespoons minced green
  onions with part of green tops

4 tablespoons lightly toasted
  pine nuts
2 tablespoons moist dried
  currants
Bengal dressing (recipe below)
Salt to taste
2 or 3 hard-cooked eggs, peeled
  and cut into wedges
Ripe olives

Break lobster into small pieces in a mixing bowl. Add lemon juice, celery, water chestnuts, pineapple, chutney, onions, pine nuts, and currants, and toss lightly to mix. Prepare Bengal dressing. Toss salad with enough Bengal dressing to moisten well. Correct seasoning with salt. Heap salad into 4 serving plates. Top each with a spoonful of dressing. Garnish with eggs and olives. Makes 4 luncheon salads.

Bengal dressing Combine in a mixing bowl 9 tablespoons mayonnaise, 3 tablespoons commercial sour cream, and 3 tablespoons fresh coconut cream (recipe page 81) or frozen and thawed unsweetened coconut milk. Whisk or beat until smooth and blended, gradually adding about 1 tablespoon curry powder.

Tahitian Crab Salad

There probably aren't any crabs in Tahiti. But this is just an ordinary crab salad with a little twist, so it has a new name.

Make a crab salad by tossing together flaked crab meat, enough thinly slivered water chestnuts or finely diced *jícama* to give it a little crunch, a very few minced green onions, mayonnaise, salt and freshly ground black pepper to taste, and just enough rinsed and drained minced Chinese sweet red ginger to give it some flecks of color and a suspicion of a taste of ginger. Serve it on a bed of lettuce. Garnish with lemon wedges. Decorate additionally as you wish.

Fancy Crab Salad

Cut a chilled ripe papaya in half and scoop out the seeds. Sprinkle the cut surfaces with lemon juice. Make a crab salad by tossing together crab meat, finely sliced celery, and a few minced green onions with Wasabi-Watercress Dressing or Mustard-Watercress Dressing (page 92) and salt and freshly ground black pepper to taste. Pile the salad into papaya halves. Garnish with watercress sprigs and lemon wedges. Makes 2 servings.

Crab Salad in Lime Jello-O

Every Sunday when I was a kid, my mother and father and aunt and uncle used to eat together—first at one guy's house and then at the next guy's house. I was too young then to know anything about food. But one salad I always liked and hoped they'd have was this one. It's awful pretty and tastes awful good.

Make a crab salad just as usual, with flaked crab, a little onion, celery, mayonnaise, salt, and freshly ground black pepper. Make up a package of lime-flavored Jell-O and squeeze in some lemon juice for additional tartness. For each serving: pour a little of the Jell-O into the bottom of an individual cup-like mold and let it set. Then pour in a little more Jell-O and pack the mold full of crab salad and chill it. Before the soft Jell-O sets, it works itself up through the crab salad. When it's time to serve, unmold the salad, thin out a little mayonnaise with a little sour cream, pour it over the top, and garnish with lettuce leaves. Now keep this chilled until you serve it. Don't go setting it out on a buffet table in the sun, or it'll melt and get all crappy.

Salmon Mousse

1½ envelopes (1½ tablespoons) unflavored gelatin
½ cup cold water
¼ cup fresh lemon juice
½ cup mayonnaise
About ½ teaspoon dried dill weed
¼ teaspoon paprika
About ⅛ teaspoon salt
Dash of Tabasco

½ cup chopped celery
1 can (1 pound) salmon
1 cup half and half (half milk and half cream)
Lettuce leaves
Watercress sprigs and lemon wedges
Commercial sour cream, lightly salted and stirred until smooth

Sprinkle gelatin over cold water in a small saucepan. Place over low heat, and stir constantly until gelatin granules dissolve, about 3 minutes. Remove from heat and cool slightly; pour into blender container. Add lemon juice. Whirl at high speed for about 40 seconds. Add mayonnaise, dill, paprika, salt, Tabasco, and celery, and whirl until thoroughly blended. Drain salmon, remove large bones and skin, and roughly flake the salmon. Add salmon to blender mixture. Whirl until blended. Add half and half, and blend again until smooth. Pour into a lightly oiled 1-quart mold or small individual molds. Cover and chill until set. At serving time, unmold on lettuce leaves. Garnish with watercress and lemon wedges. Pass sour cream as dressing. Makes 6 to 8 servings.

Bourbon Oranges with Watercress

This is a combination salad and dessert. Use plenty of sugar; these oranges should be sweet.

6 slicing oranges
About 1½ cups unsifted powdered sugar

About ½ cup blended bourbon
Watercress sprigs

Cut peel from oranges, removing all white membrane. Slice thinly. Arrange slices in a shallow glass bowl, sprinkling each layer generously with enough powdered sugar to sweeten and with bourbon. Cover and chill for 3 to 24 hours. Generously border with watercress sprigs. Makes 6 servings.

Crepes

I'm a crepe fan.

Gosh, when we first started out, I had a secretary named Kay Grove, and she was a home economy gal before she was a secretary. In those days, the restaurant wasn't open for lunch, only for dinner. So about 11:30 in the morning, Kay and I would go out to the restaurant kitchen and make crepes—all kinds—with jelly, with marmalade, with jam. And then sometimes we got fancy and made 'em with crab and chicken.

So crepes have always been kinda special to me. Here are some recipes for some of them, starting with a recipe for basic crepes.

Crepes

3 eggs
6 tablespoons flour
⅜ teaspoon salt

1 cup milk
Butter

Beat eggs slightly. Add flour and salt and beat until smooth. Gradually add milk, beating until batter is smooth. (If possible, cover and chill for 1 hour; stir to blend well before using.) Heat butter (about ½ teaspoon for each crepe) over medium-high heat in a 7- to 8-inch crepe pan. Pour in about 3 tablespoons batter; quickly tilt and rotate pan so batter covers bottom. When lightly brown on bottom, turn and lightly brown on second side. Slip onto plate or clean towel. Makes about 12 crepes.

French Pancakes

For a luncheon without going to a lot of fuss and making chicken and crab and other fancy crepes: Just do like we used to, as I told you earlier, and take some orange marmalade and some currant jelly and some blackberry jam and some strawberry jam. Fill a few crepes with each of these different things and roll 'em up and just put 'em in a pile on a plate, and sprinkle with some powdered sugar. Then one time you eat a currant jelly one, next time a marmalade one, next a strawberry one. That'll fill your belly, and with coffee it makes a fabulous lunch.

Trader Vic's Fancy Crepes

Fancy crepe means it's fancy in flavor, in looks, and everything else. And this, fellas, is fancy. Just take time out and make this and you'll see what I mean.

12 crepes (recipe page 101)
2 tablespoons finely chopped shallots
2 tablespoons butter
¾ pound completely lean pork, ground
2 cups finely chopped cooked spinach
2 ounces prosciutto, finely chopped
½ cup finely chopped pistachio nuts
4 teaspoons minced fresh parsley

1 teaspoon crumbled dried sweet basil
½ teaspoon ground nutmeg
1 clove garlic, minced or mashed
½ pound natural mozzarella cheese, shredded
Salt and freshly ground black pepper
Parmesan topping sauce (recipe below)

Prepare crepes, set aside. In a frying pan, sauté shallots in butter just until heated through. Stir in pork, spinach, prosciutto, ¼ cup of the pistachios, parsley, basil, and nutmeg, and sauté over medium heat until pork is cooked through, about 5 minutes. Stir in garlic. Cool. Mix in cheese. Correct seasoning with salt and pepper. Spread each crepe almost to edge with one-twelfth of the spinach mixture. Roll up, folding in ends. Place crepes, side by side, in a buttered shallow baking dish. Prepare Parmesan topping sauce. Pour sauce evenly over crepes. Bake 425° oven for 5 minutes or until heated through and bubbling. Sprinkle with remaining pistachios. Makes 6 servings.

Parmesan topping sauce   Combine in a saucepan 2 cups cream sauce (recipe below), ½ cup chicken broth, and ½ cup grated Parmesan cheese. Heat to boiling, whisking until smooth. Remove from heat, and whisk in 2 tablespoons Hollandaise Sauce (recipe page 44). Whip 2 tablespoons heavy cream and fold in.

Cream sauce   Melt 4 tablespoons butter in a heavy saucepan over medium heat. Add 4 tablespoons flour and ½ teaspoon salt and cook and stir to make a smooth paste. Remove from heat, and gradually whisk in 2 cups milk, returning pan to heat to cook and whisk sauce until smooth and thickened. Cook, stirring, for 5 minutes more. Makes about 2 cups.

Ham and Morel Crepes

To make the crepe not quite so morelly, you might try adding some white whole-kernel corn. You'd have to cook it first, or use a good canned kind, drained. Add maybe about 2 teaspoons per serving. This will make this thing awfully good.

8 crepes (recipe page 101)
2 ounces dried morels
2 tablespoons minced fresh onions
½ cup butter
½ pound well smoked lean ham, diced
¼ cup dry white table wine
Morel-cream sauce (recipe below)
Salt and freshly ground black pepper
⅓ cup Hollandaise Sauce (recipe page 44)
⅓ cup heavy cream, whipped

Prepare crepes, set aside. Rinse, wash, and shake morels well in cold water to loosen all particles. Then soak in enough cold water to cover until soft throughout. Drain, saving liquid. Thinly slice. In a large frying pan, sauté onions in butter until limp. Stir in morels, ham, and wine. Cook until wine reduces by half. Prepare morel-cream sauce. Stir in ½ cup of the morel-cream sauce and heat through; correct seasoning with salt and pepper. Spread each crepe almost to edge with one-eighth of the morel mixture. Roll up, folding in ends. Arrange crepes, side by side, in a buttered shallow baking dish. Prepare Hollandaise Sauce. Fold Hollandaise and whipped cream into remaining morel-cream sauce; turn evenly over crepes. Place under broiler at least 5 inches from heat until crepes are heated through and topping is lightly browned. Makes 4 servings.

Morel-cream sauce   Melt 3 tablespoons butter in a heavy saucepan over medium heat. Add 3 tablespoons flour and ⅜ teaspoon salt and cook and stir to make a smooth paste. Remove from heat, and gradually whisk in 1 cup milk and ½ cup morel liquid, returning pan to heat to cook, and whisk sauce until smooth and thickened. Cook, stirring, for 3 to 5 minutes more.

Note: You can make and fill crepes ahead of time. If you do so, finish this way: Dot crepes lightly with butter and bake in a 350° oven until heated through, about 10 minutes. Spoon on sauce and slip under broiler until lightly browned.

Shrimp Crepes with Booze

I've heard about guys taking a massage and using bourbon instead of alcohol. And I've heard of rubbing horses with bourbon. But I never heard too much about cooking with bourbon until someone asked me to do a magazine article on bourbon cooking. And I found out that you can do a helluva lot of nice things with bourbon.

Now some of you fellas might be straight bourbon fans. But don't use straight bourbon in cooking; use blended. And while I'm at it, let me tell you that you'll be a lot better off if you make your mixed bourbon drinks with blended, not straight bourbon.

5. Bongo Bongo soup

6. Belgian endive

7. Tahitian ice cream

8. Trader Vic's wine cup

Now I have nothing against straight bourbon, but blended is just better for cooking and for mixed drinks.

This is an awfully nice little thing where bourbon is used instead of the usual brandy.

8 crepes	**2 tablespoons blended bourbon**
1 tablespoon minced shallots	**1 cup commercial sour cream**
1 teaspoon paprika	**Salt and freshly ground black**
5 tablespoons butter	**pepper**
1 pound tiny cooked and shelled	**Chopped watercress and**
shrimp	**watercress sprigs**

Prepare crepes, set aside. In a heavy frying pan, sauté shallots and paprika in 4 tablespoons of the butter until shallots are translucent. Add shrimp and turn to coat with butter. Add bourbon at edge of pan, and ignite. Spoon flaming liquid over shrimp until flames die. Remove from heat. Stir in 1 cup sour cream. Correct seasoning with salt and pepper. Spread each crepe with one-eighth of the shrimp mixture and roll up, folding in ends. Arrange crepes, side by side, in a shallow buttered baking dish, seam side down. Dot with remaining butter. Bake in a 350° oven until heated through, about 10 minutes. Sprinkle with chopped watercress and garnish with watercress sprigs. Pass additional sour cream to spoon over crepes if desired. Makes 4 servings.

THE ODD THINGS

When I say the odd things, I don't mean queer.

When I'm writing a book, I have a little of this and a little of that that I want to put in. And some of it doesn't fit anywhere. Or maybe after I've put together all of the other chapters, I think of something else, and I don't want to bust in and break the chapters all up. Those are the things that are here.

Maybe there's more good stuff in this chapter than in any other —so far as things that are fun to do.

Tahitian Tuna Roll

Tahitian roll. This is about as Tahitian as St. Louis. But I made this up years ago, and I think it's the best-tasting thing I ever did. It's fantastic, and your guests will like it. Keep 'em coming. Don't let 'em pile up and get cold on you.

You can do this same thing with chicken salad or ham salad or a salad made of chopped-up hot dogs. Don't be afraid to experiment. Now you can munch on one of these and drink beer or whatever. Nobody else does this.

The paper wrap keeps the seafood salad from drying out as it heats and the bun crisps. If you don't have parchment paper, you can use the crisp paper that your butcher wraps hamburger up in.

2 cans (about 7 ounces each) chunk tuna, lightly drained

3 to 4 tablespoons fresh lemon juice

3 to 4 tablespoons finely chopped chowchow (mustard pickles)

1 cup finely chopped celery

4 teaspoons minced fresh parsley

4 teaspoons minced green onions with part of green tops

4 teaspoons minced green bell peppers

Mayonnaise

Salt and freshly ground black pepper

2 large hot dog buns

Flake tuna. Add lemon juice, chowchow, celery, parsley, onions, and peppers. Mix thoroughly, then toss with enough mayonnaise to moisten well. Season with salt and pepper. Split hot dog buns, and hollow out the soft centers to leave a shell. Pile tuna mixture lightly into each shell. Roll-wrap each in a sheet of parchment paper so that seam or end is on bottom. Place on baking sheet. Bake in a 400° oven for 6 to 8 minutes or until salad is heated through and buns are crisp. Serve right in paper on plate. Makes 4 rolls.

Tahitian Crab or Shrimp Roll

½ pound flaked crab meat or tiny cooked and shelled shrimp

1½ tablespoons fresh lemon juice

1 cup finely chopped celery

2 tablespoons minced green onions with part of green tops

2 hard-cooked eggs, finely chopped

Mayonnaise

1 teaspoon Dijon-style mustard

¼ teaspoon Worcestershire sauce

Salt and freshly ground black pepper

2 large hot dog buns

Combine crab or shrimp, lemon juice, celery, onions, and eggs in a bowl. Stir together 3 tablespoons mayonnaise, the mustard, and

Worcestershire sauce to make a dressing. Toss crab mixture with enough dressing to moisten well; if necessary, add a little more mayonnaise. Season to taste with salt and pepper. Split hot dog buns, and hollow out the soft centers to leave a shell. Pile crab mixture lightly into each shell. Roll-wrap each in a sheet of parchment paper so that end of paper is on bottom. Place on baking sheet. Bake in a 400° oven for 6 to 8 minutes or until salad is heated through and buns are crisp. Serve right in paper on plate. Makes 4 rolls.

Shrimp or Crab or Chicken Buns

Start with the best shrimp or crab or chicken salad you can make. Split nice big fat hot dog buns, and hollow out the soft centers to leave a shell. Brush the shells with melted butter and broil quickly until golden and crisp. Immediately line the shells with a little leaf lettuce, fill with chilled shrimp or crab or chicken salad, and serve.

Potato Chip Sandwich

Potato chip sandwich sounds crazy as hell. But if you like peanut butter—this is a helluva way to eat it. You crunch down on potato chips, and believe me, fellows, it's a lot of fun. Add some crisp bacon if you feel like it.

2 slices white sandwich bread	**Whole potato chips**
Mayonnaise	**Crisply cooked bacon slices**
Peanut butter	**(optional)**
Crisp lettuce	

Spread 1 bread slice thickly with mayonnaise. Spread other slice thickly with peanut butter; top with a layer of lettuce, then a layer of potato chips, and then, if you wish, a layer of bacon. Close sandwich. Cut off bread crusts if you wish. Cut diagonally to make 2 sandwiches.

Pancakes My Dad's Way

Gosh, these were good! My dad worked in San Francisco as a waiter in 1910 and around that time, and we only saw him on Saturdays and Sundays every two weeks. He'd come home every night so late that we'd all be asleep and he'd leave early in the morning. But on Saturday and Sunday, he'd make his pancakes or ham and eggs (recipe page 73).

He'd make a regular pancake batter and add thinly sliced, peeled apples or fresh peaches or little flake pieces of pineapple, then fry the pancakes. This is the most! Now remember that the fruit must be sliced paper-thin. *Sprinkle* the slices into the bowl of batter or they'll all stick in a glob. Dip out and bake pancakes. Maybe one pancake has one apple slice, maybe one has three. That's more fun for the guy who gets three. Boy, this isn't much trouble, and it sure helps pancakes a lot.

When I was a kid, we didn't get buttermilk very often. But once in a while we did, and then my mother would make buttermilk pancakes, and they're really better than the sweet milk ones.

We topped these with melted butter and sugar or syrup.

1 egg	1 teaspoon sugar
1½ cups buttermilk	1 teaspoon baking powder
½ teaspoon vanilla	½ teaspoon baking soda
2 tablespoons melted butter or salad oil	½ teaspoon salt
1¼ cups sifted all-purpose flour	About 1 cup very thinly sliced apples or fresh peaches or pineapple

In a mixing bowl, beat egg. Beat in buttermilk, vanilla, and butter. Sift remaining ingredients except fruit together into bowl, and beat just until all flour is moistened; batter will be a little lumpy. Sprinkle in fruit and mix in. Spoon batter onto lightly buttered griddle or heavy skillet over medium or medium-high heat, making about 4-inch circles. When the top side is full of bubbles, turn pancakes and brown on second side. Makes about 16 pancakes.

Red Flannel Hash

All right. This is corned beef hash—with a twist that tastes and looks good. It's an old New England dish and well worth the effort.

This is mainly for brunch. But you can make it for breakfast or even dinner. You can top each serving with a poached or softly fried egg.

¼ pound lean salt pork with
rind removed, cut into ¼-inch
dice
½ cup finely chopped onions
Butter
3 cups diced, cooked potatoes
2 cups (½ pound) finely
chopped, cooked lean corned
beef

1¼ cups diced cooked beets
(fresh or canned)
¼ cup heavy (whipping) cream
¼ cup chopped fresh parsley
Salt and pepper to season

In a large frying pan, sauté salt pork and onions in about 3 table-spoons butter until golden. Add remaining ingredients and mix well. Push mixture to side of pan, add a generous amount of butter, and let it melt. Spread mixture evenly over pan and press down firmly. Fry over medium and low heat until crisp and brown on bottom, about 15 minutes. Then lift sections with a pancake turner, add more butter as needed, turn, and brown well on other side, about 15 minutes more. Makes 6 to 8 servings.

Tomato Gravy Maryland

I have some friends, a guy by the name of Sturgis Wells and his bride, Katie, who used to live in Harford County, Maryland. That was a thousand years ago. They used to entertain a lot at Sunday breakfast, and they did some damn good things.

Here is what they did with tomatoes. Sounds crazy as hell, but they say it's good.

Take 3 or 4 strips of bacon per person and fry very crisp in a heavy skillet. Remove and keep warm. Leave a moderate amount of bacon fat in skillet. Thickly slice ripe tomatoes and fry over medium-high heat in same skillet, adding salt and freshly ground black pepper and a tiny sprinkling of sugar; turn once; fry until the liquid disappears and the tomatoes are brown. Remove tomatoes from skillet. Add to skillet ½ cup or more scalded milk per person. Cook and stir, loosening drippings, until milk is reduced by about one third. Season with salt and pepper. Lay tomato slices on buttered toast, pour milk gravy over, and lay bacon slices on top. This is great for brunch or supper.

Fried Peaches Maryland

Here's what they did to peaches.

Fry 3 or 4 strips of bacon per person. Remove and keep warm. Leave a generous amount of bacon fat in skillet. Peel, halve, and pit half-ripe fresh peaches. Over medium heat, lightly sauté peaches in bacon drippings in skillet, turning several times, sprinkling with brown sugar after each turning, and spooning syrup over peaches. You sauté until all the juices cook down to almost a candy consistency. When peaches are crisp and golden brown, they are done. Drain them well, lay on warm plates, put strips of bacon over, and serve. Great for brunch.

Baltimore Kidneys

They did this with kidneys. Buy the pinkest kidneys you can find; the lighter the kidney is in color, the milder it is.

Remove membrane and core from veal or beef kidneys. Cut into small bite-sized pieces. Cover with well-salted cold water and allow to soak for about a half hour. Drain and rinse in clear water. Put kidneys into a large frying pan with cold water to cover, and with chopped celery leaves, minced onions, and bay to season. Heat to boiling. Remove from heat and skim off scum from top. Cover and simmer until kidneys are tender, about 5 to 15 minutes. Stir together 1½ tablespoons soft butter and 1½ tablespoons flour for each 2 cups of hot kidney liquid. Stirring constantly, add to bubbling liquid in skillet. Cook and gently stir until liquid is smooth and slightly thickened. Season well with Worcestershire sauce, salt, and freshly ground black pepper. Serve over buttered crisp waffles or toast.

Dumplings

There are several ways to make dumplings, but this is the way I like 'em.

I use Bisquick, and I don't follow the formula on the box. They say to cook dumplings for twenty minutes; I cook mine for forty minutes. I use milk and I don't measure; I use less than they say on the package; I just pour in enough milk so it looks like it will work. I make my dumplings bigger than they do.

Now when you mix or stir, do it lightly. For God's sake, fellows, handle the dough as if it were gonna blow up any minute. Handle it very softly with your fingers or a fork, and just mix up the dough very slightly and handle it gently. Now if you find a lump in there, press it out of course. But don't go beating all of the air out of it. If you stir too much, you will beat all the air out and your dumplings won't rise. The dough should be a little softer than biscuit dough—not much.

Now you get a big serving spoon, fill it, and run your finger down it to dump the stuff onto your bubbling broth or gravy. *Don't* just dump the dough into plain water; the dumplings will turn out tasting awful. Don't put in too many dumplings. Place them so they float easy and have some space to puff up in. Then you put on the lid and steam them. Now once you have them in the pot, don't go sticking your nose in every few minutes. Keep the lid on and don't peek for forty minutes. Now don't forget, forty minutes instead of twenty like it says on the box. There's where the Bisquick guys make their mistake; the damn dumplings aren't cooked enough in twenty minutes. And don't have the fire too hot. The liquid should be just bubbling lightly. The dumplings need lots of steam to cook.

Now if you want to make your dumplings oh-so-good peachy: Take some hamburger and brown it and add it to your dough along with a little thyme or rosemary. Or season your dumplings with nutmeg. Or chop up some cooked sausage into little pieces and add it to your dough. Or another idea—this'll kill you. Take a handful of shelled pistachios and boil them for ten minutes in lightly salted water. Slip off the brown peels. Cut each nut in half. Put them in the dumpling dough. It'll taste like you're eating boiled fingernails.

My Dumplings

2 cups Bisquick
Milk

Put Bisquick into a bowl. Gradually pour in less than ⅔ cup milk, mixing very lightly with a fork or fingers. The mixture should be lumpy, not smooth. Makes 8 dumplings.

Cheese Polenta

If you want to be fancy, moisten several layers of cheesecloth in hot water, wring out, and use it to form the polenta into a shape: just press the cheesecloth down over the polenta and pat it into shape—before you add the topping layer of cheese. Remove cheesecloth. Put on the top cheese. Carve polenta at the table. For something even more fantastic: put some of those boiled pistachios (as in the preceding recipe) into your polenta after it's cooked.

Make polenta (recipe below). When the polenta is cooked, spread half of it over the bottom of a warm deep platter. Top it with slices of Teleme or soft Monterey Jack cheese and a sprinkling of grated Parmesan. Top it with the remaining polenta, more slices of Teleme, and a little Parmesan. Be sure that this is good and hot, and serve immediately—while the cheese is melting in.

Polenta   In the top part of a double boiler over direct heat, bring 2½ cups chicken broth to a boil. Mix 1 cup polenta or yellow corn meal with 1½ cups chicken broth and add to the boiling broth. Reduce heat, and cook, stirring, until the mixture boils. Place over boiling water in bottom of a double boiler and cook, covered, for about 45 minutes, stirring occasionally. Season to taste with freshly ground black pepper and salt if necessary. Makes about 6 servings.

Old-Fashioned Country Gravy

Here's how you make real old-fashioned country gravy. You use it on any meat that's been browned in a skillet and that doesn't have its own gravy.

Goddammit, more sins are committed making this than any other gravy. When you make it right, this is fabulous.

If you want to fudge a little bit, you can add a *little* beef concentrate such as Bovril. That'll bring the flavor up. But don't add too much or it'll louse it all up.

Fry your meat (pork, ham, veal, beef, chicken) in your usual way in an old-fashioned heavy iron skillet. Remove meat and keep warm. For about 2 cups gravy: Add butter to drippings in skillet to make 4 tablespoons. Add 4 tablespoons flour, and cook and stir over medium heat to make a smooth paste and to lightly brown flour. Remove from heat and gradually add 2 cups milk (or more if you want a thinner gravy), returning to heat and stirring between additions. Cook and stir for about 3 to 5 minutes more to make a smooth sauce. Season well with salt and freshly ground black pepper.

Green Enchiladas

1 can (10½ ounces) cream of
mushroom soup

3 cans (4 ounces each) Ortega
green chiles

6 corn tortillas (each about 7
inches in diameter)

Water

About ½ pound Monterey Jack
cheese, cut into 6 strips, each
about 5 by ¾ by ¾ inch

About ¾ cup commercial sour
cream

Sliced ripe olives and/or thinly
sliced green onions with part
of green tops

Strain mushrooms out of soup. Put strained soup and contents of 1 can of chiles into blender; whirl until smooth. Lightly brush each tortilla on both sides with water, then place flat on an ungreased heavy frying pan or griddle over medium heat, and turn until soft and pliable, heating only about 15 seconds on each side. To make each enchilada: Put a strip of cheese into one seeded chile from remaining cans. Dip 1 tortilla into mushroom sauce, and roll around the cheese-stuffed chile. Repeat to use all chiles. Place enchiladas, side by side, seam side down, in a single layer in an oiled shallow baking dish. Pour remaining mushroom sauce evenly over. Bake in a 350° oven for 20 minutes or until bubbling. Stir sour cream until smooth, then spoon a little down the length of each enchilada. Sprinkle with olives and/or onions. Makes 6 enchiladas.

Señor Pico Presidio Chili

Yes, yes—chili with beans, chili with meat, chili with chili, anything you want to do with chili is OK with me. The most important thing in making good chili is to go and find yourself some good chili powder.

I was reading an article recently done by some donkey who thinks he is a food writer, and he says that he has a whole bunch of recipes calling for two teaspoonfuls of chili powder. Well, I flipped my cork. Two teaspoons means nothing when it comes to chili powder. Chili powder is like a Yo-Yo; there are all different kinds. A half teaspoonful of one kind might have the punch of two tablespoons of another kind. The chili powder you get in the grocery store tastes terrible.

At our Señor Pico restaurants, we make our own chili powder. You need good ground chili to begin with.

1 pound dry red kidney beans, well rinsed	1 bay leaf
Water	About 2 tablespoons chili powder
3 tablespoons crumbled large dried mild red chilis (such as ancho, pasilla, or California)	½ teaspoon crumbled dried oregano
½ pound ground chuck	1 can (10 ounces) Las Palmas red chili sauce
½ pound finely diced lean pork	Salt
⅓ cup salad oil	1 cup whole kernels cut from fresh corn or drained canned whole-kernel corn
1 large onion, finely chopped	
1 large clove garlic, minced or mashed	

Put beans into a large kettle, and add cold water to cover generously. Cover and heat to boiling, boil for 2 minutes, remove from heat, and let stand for 1 hour. Drain, saving liquid. Rinse and drain chilis, cover with hot water, let soak for 1 hour, then drain, saving liquid. In a large, heavy kettle, lightly brown beef and pork in oil. Add onions, and sauté until limp. Stir in chilis, beans, and remaining ingredients except salt and corn. Combine liquid drained from chilis and beans, add enough water to measure 6 cups; add to kettle. Cover and simmer, stirring occasionally, until beans are almost tender, about 1 hour. Add 1 teaspoon salt, cover, and simmer until beans are tender, about 30 minutes more. Correct seasoning. Add corn just before serving; fresh corn should simmer for about 5 minutes, canned corn should just heat through. Makes about 8 servings.

Pake Noodles

Now you can serve noodles till hell won't have 'em—boiled, fried, every old way. But these noodles are special. They are noodles cooked Chinese style. You've got to do them right, just according to the recipe. Try this sometime on your old lady. Then the next time, do it for your guests.

Cook medium-sized egg noodles (fresh or packaged dry) in boiling salted water until just tender (*al dente*), rinse, and drain well. Measure 2 cups. In a frying pan, sauté noodles in ⅓ cup melted butter until heated through. Sprinkle with about ½ teaspoon salt, a generous grinding of black pepper, 2 tablespoons fine dry bread crumbs, and 1½ tablespoons toasted sesame seeds. Sauté until heated through and mixed. Makes 3 to 4 servings.

Rice Noodles

You buy transparent rice noodles, labeled rice sticks or *py mei fun* or *my fun,* in an Oriental grocery store. Soak them in warm water for about 1 hour. Drain. Melt plenty of butter in a frying pan over medium heat. Add noodles and enough water to moisten well and toss just until they're heated through and cloaked with butter and tender. But don't cook them long; if you do, you'll cook 'em right out of existence. Season with salt and freshly ground black pepper and a little soy sauce if you like it, or with salt and pepper and browned butter (in this case, sauté in less butter and a little more water).

Rice Roberta

The vegetables should be chopped to the consistency of coffee grounds. And don't try to cook them; follow the recipe. You cook the rice just tender and rinse and drain it well before you start.

3 cups cooked long-grain white
  rice
½ teaspoon salt
¼ teaspoon white pepper
⅓ cup butter
1½ cups extremely finely
  chopped celery

1½ cups extremely finely
  chopped carrots
2 tablespoons minced fresh
  parsley or snipped chives

In a heavy frying pan, sauté rice, salt, and pepper in butter until heated through. Fold in celery, carrots, and parsley and *just* heat through; do not cook. Serve immediately. Makes 6 servings.

Ravioli and Quick Cheese Sauce with Soy

Get freshly made ravioli for this if you can.

6 dozen ravioli pieces
Cheese-ham sauce (recipe below)
⅓ to ½ cup finely chopped, lightly toasted pistachio nuts

Cook ravioli just until tender (*al dente*) in a generous amount of boiling salted water. Drain well. Prepare cheese-ham sauce. Fold ravioli into cheese-ham sauce. Turn into a warm serving dish or serving plates. Sprinkle with pistachios. Makes 6 servings.

Cheese-ham sauce   In a saucepan or deep frying pan, melt 1 tablespoon butter. Stir in 1 tablespoon flour to make a smooth paste. Gradually add ¾ cup milk, cooking and stirring to make a smooth and thickened sauce. Gradually add 2 cups half and half (half milk and half cream), and cook and stir for about 5 minutes more to make a thin sauce. Reduce heat to low and stir in 2 ounces finely diced cooked smoked ham, 2 ounces shredded natural sharp Cheddar cheese, and 1 teaspoon Kikkoman soy sauce. Heat, stirring, until cheese melts and sauce is smooth. Correct seasoning with salt and freshly ground black pepper.

Tortellini Trader

4 tablespoons butter

2 cups heavy (whipping) cream

½ teaspoon ground nutmeg

½ cup finely diced prepared sweetbreads (recipe page 19)

4 dozen pieces tortellini, preferably fresh (or use frozen), cooked just until tender (al dente) in boiling salted water and drained

¼ pound well-smoked cooked ham, cut into fine julienne strips

1 egg yolk, beaten

About ¾ cup grated Parmesan cheese

About ⅓ cup finely chopped, lightly toasted pistachio nuts

In a large frying pan, heat butter, cream, and nutmeg to boiling. Add sweetbreads, tortellini, and half of the ham, and bring quickly to boiling, stirring to mix. Mix a little of the hot sauce with the egg yolk. Remove pan from heat, and stir in yolk mixture and the Parmesan. Turn into warm casserole for serving or serve onto warm plates. Sprinkle with remaining ham and the pistachios. Makes 4 servings.

Galette de St.-Germain-des-Prés

When he was young, my old man lived in the backwoods of Canada, up out of Ste. Anne de Beaupré. It got so cold there at night that they just hung the butter from a piece of string from the ceiling, over the dining room table. Whenever anyone wanted butter on his bread, he'd just reach over and get ahold of the butter and rub it over the bread. If somebody wanted it at the other end of the table, they'd shoot it down to him. Well, now, that's pretty cold.

His family used to make a thing called a *galette*. It's French. (My father's family was French; they left France at the time the Huguenots were getting their heads chopped off by the Catholics.) It was a complicated bread dough thing, and they made it when they were baking a big batch of bread.

Then it was complicated, but here's the easy way to do it now.

These are good for breakfast with fresh raspberries and hot chocolate.

½ cup sugar	3 tablespoons melted butter
½ teaspoon ground cinnamon	2 rolls from a package of
¼ teaspoon ground nutmeg	Pillsbury butterflake dinner
⅛ teaspoon ground cloves	rolls

Stir together sugar, cinnamon, nutmeg, and cloves; stir in butter. On a lightly floured board, roll out each roll to a 5-inch circle. Place well apart on an ungreased baking sheet; stretch and press dough down onto sheet to hold in place. Sprinkle half of the sugar mixture onto each circle—within ¾ inch of the edge. Bake in a 400° oven for 12 minutes or until rich golden brown. Slip onto a wire rack to cool. Makes 2 galettes.

Extra-Fancy Galette de St.-Germain-des-Prés

⅓ cup moist pitted dates (press firmly to measure), cut into small pieces	½ teaspoon ground cinnamon
	¼ cup butter
¼ cup finely chopped pecans	2 rolls from a package of
½ cup sugar	Pillsbury butterflake dinner
	rolls

Mix dates, nuts, sugar, and cinnamon; stir in butter. Follow directions in above recipe to roll out packaged rolls, and place on baking sheet. Sprinkle half of the date mixture onto each circle—within ¾ inch of the edge. Bake and cool as above. Makes 2 galettes.

POMP and SPLENDOR

Pomp and splendor, pomp and splendor. Pomp and splendor can be all kinds of fancy stuff, and it can be all kinds of crappy stuff.

But when you do pomp and splendor, do it so it tastes good. It should look nice, too. But let's have none of this big poom-poom-pee-doo to make a big presentation of something that turns out to taste like nothing.

Here's a bunch of stuff that is a little more involved than some other recipes in the book, and that really tastes good.

My Cassoulet

With red wine and salad, this makes a sonofabitch of a meal.

4 lamb shanks, cracked
Salt and freshly ground black
  pepper
Flour
1 pound dry small white (navy)
  beans, rinsed
Water
2 medium-sized onions, chopped
1 large can (1 pound 12 ounces)
  tomatoes

2 large cloves garlic, minced or
  mashed
1 large bay leaf
2 tablespoons dry white table
  wine
¾ pound knackwurst (Swiss or
  German garlic sausages),
  casings removed if necessary

Wipe shanks dry. Season generously with salt and pepper; coat with flour and shake off excess. Place in a greased baking pan. Cover and bake in a 350° oven until lamb is tender, about 2 hours. Meantime, put beans into a large (6-quart or more) casserole. Add 5 cups cold water. Cover and heat to boiling, boil for 2 minutes, remove from heat, and let stand for 1 hour. Stir in onions, tomatoes, garlic, bay leaf, and ¾ teaspoon pepper. Add baked shanks. Cover and bake in a 300° oven for 1½ hours or until beans are tender. Remove lamb from bones in large pieces and return to kettle. Stir in wine and 2 teaspoons salt. Cut sausages into diagonal ½-inch-thick slices, and arrange over top. Bake, uncovered, for 45 minutes more. Add salt and pepper to taste. (If necessary, add more water during cooking; the dish should be a little soupy.) Makes 6 to 8 servings.

Old-fashioned Beef Tongue Casserole (Corned)

If necessary, add more water during cooking; the dish should tumble and flow, be a little soupy—not dry. You'll have to add salt according to taste because you can never tell how salty a corned tongue is going to be. Add more cumin if you like it.

1 pound dry red kidney beans,
  well rinsed
Water
2 medium-sized onions, finely
  chopped
About ¼ cup salad oil
2 large cloves garlic, minced or
  mashed
About ½ cup finely chopped
  fresh parsley

1 bay leaf
About 1 teaspoon ground cumin
  (or chili powder)
About ½ teaspoon freshly
  ground black pepper
Cooked corned beef tongue
  (recipe below)
¾ pound knackwurst, casings
  removed if necessary
Dijon-style mustard

Put beans into a large casserole (about 5 quarts). Add 6 cups cold water. Cover and heat to boiling, boil for 2 minutes, remove from heat, and let stand for 1 hour. Sauté onions in salad oil until limp. Stir into beans along with garlic, half of the parsley, the bay leaf, cumin, and pepper. Carve tongue into ½-inch-thick slices, and tuck into beans. Cover and bake in a 300° oven until beans are nearly tender, about 1½ hours. Taste and correct seasoning. Cut sausages into diagonal ½-inch-thick slices, and arrange over top. Bake, uncovered, for 45 minutes more. Sprinkle with remaining parsley. Pass the mustard. Makes 6 to 8 servings.

Cooked corned beef tongue   Put a 3½-pound corned beef tongue into a kettle. Cover with cold water, cover, and heat to boiling, simmer for 5 minutes, and drain. Cover with cold water again, cover, heat to boiling, then simmer until tongue is tender, about 2½ hours. While hot, remove skin from tongue and trim off excess root tissue.

Lamb and Tongue Cassoulet

Allow yourself some time to do this. Be generous with the garlic and black pepper.

Judge water and salt the same as for the preceding recipe for Old-fashioned Beef Tongue Casserole (Corned).

4 lamb shanks, cracked
Salt and freshly ground black
  pepper
Flour
1 pound dry small white (navy)
  or pink beans, well rinsed
Water
2 large onions, finely chopped
2 carrots, peeled and finely
  diced
3 large cloves garlic, minced or
  mashed

1 can (1 pound) tomatoes,
  broken up
⅛ teaspoon sugar
1 large bay leaf
1 cup finely chopped fresh
  parsley
Cooked corned beef tongue
  (recipe page 123)
¼ cup dry white table wine
Dijon-style mustard

Wipe shanks dry. Season generously with salt and pepper; coat with flour and shake off excess. Place in a greased baking pan. Cover and bake in a 350° oven until lamb is tender, about 2 hours. Put beans into a large (6-quart or more) casserole. Add 6 cups cold water. Cover and heat to boiling, boil for 2 minutes, remove from heat, and let stand for 1 hour. Stir in onions, carrots, garlic, tomatoes, sugar, bay leaf, and half of the parsley. Tuck baked shanks into beans. Carve tongue into ½-inch-thick slices, and tuck into beans. Cover and bake in a 300° oven until tender, about 2 hours. Remove lamb from bones in large pieces and return to kettle. Stir in wine. Taste and correct seasoning with salt and pepper. Bake, uncovered, for 45 minutes more. Sprinkle with remaining parsley. Pass the mustard. Makes 6 to 8 servings.

Mushroom Chicken Cassoulet

3 frying chicken thighs and 3
  frying chicken drumsticks
  (about 2¼ pounds total)
Salt and freshly ground black
  pepper
Flour
About 6 tablespoons butter
1 can (14 ounces) chicken broth
1 medium-sized onion, finely
  chopped
½ cup chopped celery
1 carrot, finely diced
2 tablespoons finely chopped
  fresh parsley
2 tablespoons Italian dried
  mushrooms, soaked until
  soft, squeezed dry and
  chopped

⅓ pound fresh mushrooms,
  thinly sliced
3 ounces dried egg noodles,
  cooked al dente in boiling
  salted water and drained
1 can (1 pound) peeled whole
  tomatoes, drained and broken
  up
1 large clove garlic, minced or
  mashed
½ teaspoon crumbled dried
  rosemary
¼ teaspoon sugar
1½ teaspoons A.1. sauce
3 to 4 tablespoons dry sherry
3 to 4 tablespoons grated
  Parmesan cheese

Season chicken generously with salt and pepper; coat with flour and shake off excess. In a deep frying pan or large casserole over medium heat, brown chicken thoroughly on all sides in about 3 tablespoons of the butter. Remove to a kettle, add chicken broth, cover, and simmer until chicken is tender, about 45 minutes. Remove chicken from broth, remove meat from bones in fairly large pieces, discard bones. Add onions, celery, and carrots to chicken drippings in large frying pan and sauté until limp. Stir in parsley and dried mushrooms. In a small frying pan over medium-high heat, sauté fresh mushrooms in 2 tablespoons butter until tender. Add to sautéed vegetables along with chicken meat and broth, noodles, tomatoes, garlic, rosemary, sugar, A.1., and sherry. Correct seasoning with salt and pepper. Sprinkle with Parmesan. Dot with about 1 tablespoon butter. Bake in a 350° oven for 30 minutes or until heated through and bubbling. If necessary to brown top further, slip under broiler. Makes 6 servings.

Chicken Ginger

4 frying chicken thighs and
  4 frying chicken legs
Salt and freshly ground black
  pepper
About 4 tablespoons butter
1 medium-sized onion, finely
  chopped
¾ cup chopped celery
1 large carrot, finely chopped
⅔ cup long grain white rice
1½ cups chicken broth
½ cup scalded heavy cream
2 cloves garlic, minced or
  mashed

3 tablespoons Trader Vic
  Teriyaki Marinade & Sauce
1½ tablespoons Skippy creamy
  peanut butter
½ tablespoon fresh lemon juice
⅓ cup coarsely cut, pitted
  prunes
⅓ cup coarsely cut dried
  apricots
2 tablespoons rinsed, drained,
  and minced Chinese sweet
  red ginger
2 tablespoons finely chopped
  candied orange peel

Season chicken very generously with salt and pepper. In a deep, heavy casserole over medium heat, brown chicken well on all sides in butter; remove and set aside. Add onions, celery, and carrots to drippings in casserole, and sauté until limp. Stir in rice. Add broth, cream, garlic, teriyaki sauce, peanut butter, and lemon juice, and mix well. Stir in prunes and apricots. Tuck chicken pieces into rice. Cover and bake in a 350° oven for 45 minutes or until chicken and rice are tender. Sprinkle with ginger and orange peel. Makes 4 servings.

Oxtail Stew with Optional Sweetbreads

I used to cook five thousand oxtails for the French Government before six o'clock every morning. Well, of course my mom taught me how to cook them.

Here's a way we prepare them in our restaurant. Start with choice oxtails cut from lightweight animals. To be good, they shouldn't be more than three inches at the butt, and the fat should be white. If you have to get the larger tails, trim off as much fat as possible.

12 choice oxtails, cut apart at
  joints
Flour
About ¼ cup salad oil
3 large onions, thinly sliced
Finely chopped fresh parsley
1 pound fresh mushrooms,
  sliced
4 large carrots, peeled and
  sliced
1 cup diced celery
3 cloves garlic, minced or
  mashed
Generous dash of Tabasco

Salt to season
1 teaspoon freshly ground
  black pepper
¼ teaspoon crumbled dried
  thyme
1 large bay leaf
2 cups dry red table wine
4 tablespoons A.1. sauce
1 tablespoon Worcestershire
  sauce
Beef stock or water
Sautéed sweetbreads (recipe
  below) (optional)

Roll oxtail pieces in flour, and shake off excess. In a heavy kettle or Dutch oven, brown pieces in a small amount of oil. Add onions, and turn to coat in drippings. Add ¼ cup parsley and remaining ingredients except stock and sweetbreads. Add enough stock or water to barely cover oxtails. Heat to boiling, then cover and simmer slowly until meat is very tender, about 2½ hours; stir occasionally. Add sweetbreads, and simmer for about 30 minutes more. Correct seasoning with salt, pepper, and A.1. sauce. Sprinkle generously with additional parsley. Makes about 10 servings.

Sautéed sweetbreads   Cut 2 pounds prepared sweetbreads (double recipe page 19) into ¾-inch pieces. Sauté over medium-high heat in about 3 tablespoons butter until golden brown. Season well with salt and pepper.

Lambs' Tongues Trader Vic

1 medium-sized onion, finely
  chopped
1 cup chopped celery
1 carrot, peeled and finely
  chopped
Butter
1 large can (1 pound 12 ounces)
  peeled whole tomatoes
  (preferably Italian pear-
  shaped tomatoes), broken up
¼ cup dry white table wine

Finely chopped fresh parsley
2 cloves garlic, minced or
  mashed
¼ teaspoon sugar
Salt and freshly ground black
  pepper
Dash of Tabasco
12 prepared lambs' tongues
  (recipe below)
1 pound prepared sweetbreads
  (recipe page 19)

In a large kettle, sauté onions, celery, and carrots in 3 tablespoons butter until limp. Stir in tomatoes, wine, 1 tablespoon parsley, the garlic, sugar, ½ teaspoon salt, ¼ teaspoon pepper, and Tabasco. Add prepared tongues, cover, and simmer for about 30 minutes. Cut sweetbreads into ¾-inch pieces. In a heavy frying pan over medium-high heat, sauté sweetbreads in about 1½ tablespoons butter until golden brown; season well with salt and pepper. Add to kettle with tongues. Simmer, covered, for about 20 minutes more. Taste and correct seasoning with a generous amount of salt and pepper. Sprinkle with additional parsley. Makes 4 servings.

Prepared lambs' tongues Carefully wash and clean 12 lambs' tongues. Put into a kettle with 3 quarts cold water, 1 tablespoon salt, 1 teaspoon ground black pepper, 1 peeled and quartered onion, 1 stalk celery, 1 sprig parsley, 1 bay leaf, and 2 slices lemon. Heat to boiling, cover, and simmer until tongue is tender and outer skin strips away easily, about 1½ hours. Remove from broth, and while very hot remove skins. Cut off excess root tissue. Split lengthwise.

Lambs' Tongues, Sauce Poulette

12 lambs' tongues
⅓ pound fresh mushrooms,
  finely chopped
3 tablespoons minced green
  onions (white part only)
Butter
1 pound prepared sweetbreads
  (recipe page 19), cut into
  ¾-inch pieces
Salt and freshly ground black
  pepper

3 tablespoons flour
¾ cup milk
2 egg yolks
½ cup heavy (whipping) cream
Fresh lemon juice
Dash of Tabasco
Minced fresh parsley
About ⅛ teaspoon ground
  nutmeg (optional)
Freshly grated Parmesan cheese

Prepare lambs' tongues following recipe for Prepared lambs' tongues (recipe page 128) *except* cook tongues until very tender, and strain and save 1 cup of the broth in which tongues were cooked. In a heavy frying pan over medium-high heat, sauté mushrooms and onions in 4 tablespoons butter until tender; remove and set aside. In same frying pan over medium-high heat, sauté sweetbreads in about 1½ tablespoons butter until golden brown; season well with salt and pepper. In a large, heavy saucepan over medium heat, melt 3 tablespoons butter. Add flour and cook and stir to make a smooth paste. Remove from heat, and gradually stir in the 1 cup broth from cooking tongues and the milk, occasionally returning to heat and cooking, whisking, to make a smooth and slightly thickened sauce. Simmer, stirring, for about 3 minutes more. In a large mixing bowl, beat egg yolks with cream; gradually beat in the hot sauce. Return to saucepan and cook, whisking, just until mixture simmers. Add ½ teaspoon lemon juice, Tabasco, 2 teaspoons parsley, and nutmeg if you wish. Taste and correct seasoning with salt, pepper, and lemon juice. Add tongues, mushrooms and onions, and sweetbreads and simmer just to heat through. Turn into a warm serving platter and sprinkle lightly with Parmesan and a little more parsley. Makes 6 servings.

The SWEET TOOTH stuff

Desserts. Jeezus, they're infinite. You can put together almost any sweet combination of goofy stuff, and it'll usually turn out to be pretty good. I've tasted things that look like they'd taste horrible, and they turn out to be immaculate.

What you're looking for in dessert is something sweet. You can use cheese, fruit, ice cream, any damn thing.

Here we've brought together some desserts that aren't too usual.

Tutti-Frutti

Here is a fantastic dessert that has disappeared from the scene. My dad made this many years ago. It takes a little work, but it's worth it. It's spectacular!

First of all, you need a big, deep platter that is heatproof. It should be at least an inch and a quarter deep. I used to use a big flat dish used for flower arrangements.

You do this when the summer fruits are in season. You'll need a lot of fresh stuff—apricots, peaches, grapes, oranges, bananas, plums, cherries. You have to have cherries. But don't use berries because they stick in your teeth.

In the center of the platter, put a pile of small cocktail sugar cubes. Mound up the whole pound boxful. Then take 4 bananas, peel them, and cut them in half lengthwise and dip them in some lemon juice so they won't turn brown on you. Put 2 banana halves, cut side up, along each side of the mound of cubes—to surround the sugar. Then use all of the other fruit—quartered slices of oranges, apricots, plums, peaches, grapes—and stack them up on the bananas—to build sort of a fort all around the sugar. That fort or crown of fruit should be about 4 inches high. Secure things with toothpicks if you need to. Then put the cherries over the top of the mound of sugar to fill up the fort. They have to be big fat pitted Bing cherries. If you can't get them fresh, use frozen Bing cherries.

Now when you get ready to serve this thing, you put the whole platter with fruit into the oven to warm it through. Get a bottle of brandy, pour it into a container, and heat it just to warm. (Don't warm the brandy in the bottle, or it might explode right in your guests' faces.) And warm about a half pint of kirsch or cherry brandy, too. Then turn down your lights for some atmosphere. Bring out the platter, pour on half of the brandy, and ignite the whole damn thing. (That's why all the stuff has to be warm—so it will light—otherwise you will just be putting your matches out in it.) Then baste the fruit with the flaming brandy and the juices, and keep on adding warm brandy and cherry brandy and basting the fruit until you are tired of basting. Then break down the fort and stir it all around. Mash the whole thing and keep stirring and mashing and stirring until the fruit starts to get soft.

In the meantime, your old lady can have the demitasse coffee ready and have some liqueur glasses out and have ready some dishes of vanilla ice cream with ladyfingers stuck into it. And then you pour the wonderful juice onto everything—into the liqueur glasses, into the coffee, and along with every kind of fruit over the ice cream. The whole thing will drive you right out of your ever-lovin' mind.

Jeezus, if you are doing this thing for your girl friend, she will be so impressed, she'll propose to *you* before the fire goes out!

But be very careful with your fire. You might set your house on fire if you aren't.

Ginger Ice Cream

You know, fellows, people eat a helluva lot of ice cream. But generally, it's just the same old thing. Now try this.

Start with vanilla ice cream. Go to Chinatown or a specialty food store and get some preserved ginger in syrup; chop it up so the pieces of ginger are a little smaller than coffee beans. Stick this ginger in its syrup on top of scoops of the ice cream. And your guests'll say that you're as smart as hell.

Southern Apricot

This looks goods, smells good, and tastes good. If you want it extra special, stick a scoop of vanilla ice cream on top of the apricots before you put on the pistachios.

Halve and pit and drain some fine quality canned chilled apricot halves and arrange in stemmed dessert dishes. Dribble some Southern Comfort over them and let them marinate a little. Sprinkle with some chopped pistachio nuts.

Praline Sauce

Ladle this, warm, over rich rum or vanilla ice cream.

⅔ cup pecan halves	½ cup dark Karo corn syrup
½ cup firmly packed light brown sugar	1 tablespoon butter

Drop pecans into boiling water, and boil for 5 minutes; drain. Combine brown sugar, syrup, and butter in top part of double boiler. Place over boiling water and heat, stirring occasionally, until thoroughly blended and sugar melts. Stir in pecans. Makes topping for 4 to 5 servings.

Tahitian Ice Cream

You can buy *rhum babas* in cans.

For each serving: Place a warm individual rhum baba in a dessert plate. Top with a scoop of coconut ice cream. Ladle the following sauce over ice cream, and serve the dessert immediately: Place in a small pan 1 tablespoon pineapple-apricot jam, 1½ tablespoons light Puerto Rican rum, and 1½ teaspoons dark Jamaica rum. Heat to warm, ignite, and spoon the flaming liquid high over jam until flames die. Stir remaining liquid in pan and jam together.

Flaming Bourbon Oranges

¾ cup orange marmalade	½ cup blended bourbon
4 oranges, peeled and cut into sections, removing membrane	4 scoops hard-frozen coffee and/or vanilla ice cream (about 1 pint hand-packed)
1 tablespoon grated fresh orange peel	About 3 tablespoons lightly toasted slivered almonds (optional)
1 tablespoon grated fresh lemon peel	

Heat marmalade over low heat in a chafing dish until melted. Add oranges and orange and lemon peels, and heat just to bubbling. Add bourbon at edge of dish, heat just to warm, and light. Gently spoon flaming juices over oranges, lifting them high to allow oxygen to reach them, until flames die. Put ice cream into individual serving dishes, top with oranges and juices, sprinkle with almonds, and serve immediately. Makes 4 servings.

Baked Pears with Vanilla Butterscotch Sauce

A baked pear, for some unknown reason, to me is a very classic thing to eat. Usually they serve it with a lot of chocolate sauce flopped on it or maybe some maple syrup. Well, I served a baked pear the other night with a butterscotch sauce with a piece of vanilla bean in it, and that makes a pear really jim-dandy.

4 baking pears (Comice or Bosc)
3 tablespoons fresh lemon juice
3 tablespoons sugar
1 tablespoon butter

½ cup water
Hot vanilla butterscotch sauce
   (recipe below)

Peel, halve, and core pears. Coat pear surfaces completely with lemon juice. Arrange pears, cut side up, in a buttered shallow baking dish. Sprinkle with any remaining lemon juice and with sugar. Dot with butter. Pour water into bottom of dish. Cover tightly and bake in a 350° oven until tender, about 40 to 45 minutes. For each serving, put 2 halves in shallow dessert plates or bowls. Ladle on butterscotch sauce. Makes 4 servings.

Hot vanilla butterscotch sauce   In a saucepan, melt ½ cup butter. Scrape seeds from 1 split vanilla bean and add, along with scraped pod. Stir in 1½ cups firmly packed light brown sugar and 2 tablespoons light corn syrup. Heat to a gentle boil over medium heat and cook, stirring, until sugar melts. Gradually stir in ½ cup heavy cream and return to a boil, stirring to blend. Makes about 2 cups.

Hans's Raspberries, Old Vienna

2 pints fresh red raspberries
1½ cups heavy (whipping)
   cream

3 tablespoons granulated sugar
1 teaspoon vanilla
Raw (or dark brown) sugar

Mound berries lightly into each of 4 individual shallow stemmed dessert dishes. Beat cream with granulated sugar and vanilla until softly whipped. Spoon half of the cream on top of berries. Sprinkle each serving with 1 tablespoon raw sugar. Pass remaining cream and additional raw sugar. Makes 4 servings.

Coeur à la Crème

Maybe you've eaten this in France and maybe you haven't. I've been making this for years. When I lived in Black Point, California, recuperating from an operation, I was about six or seven years old. That was a thousand years ago. We had a cow. And my mother would take clabbered milk with cream, put it in a clean flour sack, and hang it on the water faucet overnight. And next morning, it would be cream cheese. And then we'd spoon it out, and pour some more cream on it, and put some sugar on it, and that's about the best thing you've ever put into your stomach.

Now these days, it's tough to get real clabbered milk. So here's how to do it. When you finish, you'll have a nice cake of *coeur à la crème*. Serve it with granuated sugar (vanilla sugar is best) and heavy cream. Or spoon on a little bit of red currant jelly which you've melted to a sauce and cooled, and pour on cream. And that's very good.

1 cup small-curd cottage cheese	1/16 teaspoon salt
1 large package (8 ounces) cream cheese, softened	1 cup heavy (whipping) cream
¼ teaspoon vanilla	¼ teaspoon grated fresh lemon peel

With a wooden spoon, press cottage cheese through a fine wire strainer into a bowl. Add cream cheese, vanilla, and salt, and beat with an electric beater until smooth. Gradually beat in cream, and continue beating until mixture is smooth. Fold in lemon peel. Line a heart-shaped basket (about 6 inches across) or several smaller heart-shaped porcelain molds or a 3-cup basket or shallow strainer with several layers of cheesecloth. Set mold into a deep plate. Spoon cheese into mold. Fold cheesecloth ends over cheese. Cover and chill for several hours, until firm. At serving time, open cheesecloth, invert cheese onto serving platter, remove mold, and remove cheesecloth. Cut and lift or spoon into dessert plates. Top as directed above. Makes 6 servings.

Bread Pudding with Quince Jelly

Here is a crazy dessert that's fancy but easy to do. You make some bread pudding. You spoon a glob of it into a serving bowl. And you cover it with a little quince jelly. If you want to make it even better, beat some heavy cream until it just starts to stand up, and pour that over your jelly. Damn near as good as you can get in the big restaurants.

Now for your bread, use something that's firm—farm-style white bread or what they used to call buttercrust or sweet French bread or Italian bread. Don't use a bunch of soft lousy bread. Let it dry before you use it. Be sure to put in the raisins; little bitty beautiful raisins do a lot.

If you can't get quince jelly at the Quince Jelly Store, maybe your old lady makes the stuff. Or use apple jelly. If you don't have your own recipe for bread pudding, you can use this one. It's even good without the jelly and cream.

2 cups of ½-inch dices of day-old farm-style white bread or sweet French bread or Italian bread	½ teaspoon ground cinnamon
	⅜ teaspoon ground nutmeg
	¼ teaspoon salt
	1½ teaspoons vanilla
2 eggs	2¼ cups milk
½ cup firmly packed brown sugar	½ cup seedless raisins
	Quince jelly
2 tablespoons melted butter	Heavy cream, softly whipped

Spread bread in a single layer on a tray, and let stand in the air until dry. In a bowl, slightly beat eggs. Add sugar, butter, cinnamon, nutmeg, salt, vanilla, and milk, and beat to blend. Stir in raisins and bread. Pour into a buttered 8-inch round baking dish (about 1¼ quarts). Set into a pan with hot water about 1 inch deep in bottom. Bake in a 350° oven until silver knife inserted halfway between center and outside comes out clean, about 50 ' minutes. Remove to a rack and cool to lukewarm or room temperature. Spoon into serving dishes. Top each serving with a spoonful of jelly and some whipped cream. Makes about 5 servings.

Ah Lo's Persimmon Pudding Dessert

Once upon a time, my daughter Jeanne made me her wonderful Persimmon Pudding (recipe follows). And my house man, Ah Lo, made me this great dessert.

This is an awfully easy thing to do if you have some persimmon pudding around. But if you don't, you can get a can of soft plum pudding and use that instead. Of course, Ah Lo baked the little meringues himself. But you can just as well go down to the bakery and buy them.

Put a thin slice of Jeanne's Persimmon Pudding into an individual meringue. Top with a scoop of vanilla ice cream. Makes 1 serving.

Jeanne's Persimmon Pudding

1 cup mashed ripe persimmon
  pulp
1 cup sugar
2 tablespoons melted butter
1 teaspoon vanilla
1 egg
1 cup sifted all-purpose flour
2 teaspoons baking soda

½ teaspoon salt
¼ teaspoon ground cinnamon
½ cup milk
½ cup moist seedless raisins
½ cup chopped walnuts
Whipped cream lightly
  sweetened with sugar and
  flavored with vanilla

Combine in a mixing bowl the persimmon pulp, sugar, butter, vanilla, and egg, and beat until smooth. Sift together flour, soda, salt, and cinnamon, and slowly beat into persimmon mixture. Beat in milk. Stir in raisins and walnuts. Pour into a well-buttered 5-cup mold. Cover tightly. Place on a rack over boiling water in a covered kettle, and let steam for 2 hours. Let cool in mold for 10 minutes. Gently loosen at edges and turn out of mold. Cut and serve while warm. Top with whipped cream. Makes 8 to 12 servings.

Tahitian Poë

In Tahiti, they make a crazy dessert. They bake it in an *imu* with a pig. But you can make it in a greased baking pan. It's very easy. You take a can of this and a can of that and some fresh fruit and thicken with some arrowroot. If you don't have coconut milk for the top, use vanilla ice cream. It ought to be fabulous.

1 cup firmly packed raw sugar
  or light brown sugar
5 tablespoons arrowroot
Flesh of 1 ripe papaya
1 large ripe banana, cut up
1 cup drained canned mangoes
1 can (about 13 ounces)
  crushed pineapple in heavy
  syrup

1 teaspoon fresh lemon juice
Few grains of salt
Seeds scraped from 1 split
  vanilla bean
Frozen unsweetened coconut
  milk, thawed, or vanilla ice
  cream

Stir together sugar and arrowroot. Put into blender container along with remaining ingredients except coconut milk. Whirl until smooth. Turn into a buttered 8-inch square baking pan. Bake in a 350° oven until set, about 1 hour. Cool in pan. Cut into squares. Serve at room temperature with coconut milk over the top or vanilla ice cream alongside. Makes 6 to 8 servings.

Macadamia Nut Wisp

This is a take-off on a Tahitian dish made with fruit. However, I've made it with macadamia nuts instead of fruit. Hope you like it.

4 extra-large eggs
¾ cup sugar
1⅓ cups light corn syrup
⅓ cup melted butter
3 tablespoons Trader Vic's dark Jamaica rum
1½ teaspoons vanilla

1⅓ cups finely diced macadamia nuts
Frozen unsweetened coconut milk, thawed and whipped, or whipped cream which has been lightly sweetened with sugar and flavored with vanilla

Beat together until thoroughly mixed the eggs, sugar, syrup, butter, rum, and vanilla. Stir in macadamia nuts. Turn into a buttered 8-inch square baking pan. Bake in a 375° oven for 35 to 40 minutes, just until set. Cool on a rack. Spoon into dessert dishes. Top with coconut milk or whipped cream. Makes 8 servings.

My Bride's Chocolate Fudge Pudding

Guys, sometimes you're all ready to make something that really gets you climbing the walls. Well, I like chocolate in the first place. In the second place, I like something chewy. In the third place, I like something sweet. This is all of those wrapped up. During baking, a cake mixture forms and rises to the top and a chocolate sauce settles to the bottom.

1 cup sifted all-purpose flour
2 teaspoons baking powder
¼ teaspoon salt
¾ cup granulated sugar
6 tablespoons unsifted cocoa
½ cup milk

2 tablespoons melted butter
1 cup chopped pecans or walnuts
1 cup firmly packed brown sugar
1¾ cups boiling water

Sift together into a mixing bowl the flour, baking powder, salt, granulated sugar, and 2 tablespoons of the cocoa. Stir in milk and butter. Stir in nuts. Spread evenly over bottom of a buttered 9-inch square baking pan. Mix brown sugar and remaining cocoa well; sprinkle evenly over batter. Pour hot water over all (do not stir). Bake in a 350° oven for 1 hour. Spoon out and serve while warm. Makes 9 servings.

Cheesecake Hawaiian

There's a jam made in Hawaii out of poha berries. And this jam is just fabulous. It's fabulous in crepe pancakes. And it is unbelievably good on cheesecake. So what I call cheesecake Hawaiian style would be cheesecake with poha jam on the top. I don't even think they know what cheesecake is in Hawaii.

Buy some poha jam in a specialty food store. If the jam is too thick to spoon, thin it down by stirring in a very little bit of orange juice. Buy a good cheesecake. Anybody who wants to be such a perfectionist as to make his own cheesecake is out of his mind. The only reason to make your own cheesecake—when you can buy such good ones—is to crow about it. And what is there to crow about cheesecake? Cut the cake into nice wedges and then spoon on a little poha jam.

ABOUT BOOZE
MIXING IT, STIRRING IT, SPLASHING IT ON THE WALL

I'm not going to write about martinis and highballs, because if you don't know about that sort of thing, you should learn it out of another book or by experience. What I'm going to give you here are a few different fun things.

MIXING A DRINK

You need to know this if you're making a drink out of this book or any other. You stir a martini to get as little dilution as possible. You hand-shake a sour and some fizzes to get a little more dilution and also to blend the ingredients; you can use an electric drink mixer to do the same thing for some drinks. You use a heavy blender to grind shaved ice, fruit, and liquids into one mass (or mess). Now if a drink calls for shaking, then don't go putting it into a blender because you think that's easier. Follow the recipe; that's why somebody wrote it that way in the first place.

THE MORNING AFTER—GOSH!

Now let's say this first of all. I've tended bar for twenty years, and I can tell you that there is nothing that's a sure cure. The guy who drinks Worcestershire sauce and tomato juice is making himself even sicker; and that goes for the drinks made with lemon juice, too. Oh boy, what a guy will do to his guts is fantastic!

There are about two drinks in this section that come the closest to healing: the Banana Cow and the Rum Cow. You got yourself into this, so now get yourself out—phew!

PARTY DRINKS

There are a few party drinks that you can make in batches and serve at gatherings of large groups. Make a batch of punch, a good one that everybody will like, and, hell, that's the booze you serve that night. If any of your guests gets his nose out of joint and doesn't like your drink, give him a Coke, and see how fast he starts on your punch. Punches give you a chance to go to your own party and keep the thing alive instead of standing in the kitchen making drinks. I've given you formulas here for Tahitian Rum Punch, Scorpion Punch, and Trader Vic's Wine Cup; and there are others.

Of course, maybe the best thing of all is a side table with bourbon, scotch, gin, rum, vodka, the mixes, ice, and glasses. Somebody wants a drink; let him go to the bar and make his own. What the hell? It works.

BARTENDING BASICS

You'll need to know this before you start mixing any of the drinks that follow.

Simple syrup (sometimes called bar syrup, sugar syrup, or rock candy syrup)

Rock candy syrup is Trader Vic's simple syrup. It is sold in liquor and grocery stores. It is the simple syrup used in all Trader Vic bars.

To make your own simple syrup: Combine two pounds granulated sugar and two cups water. Boil until sugar is thoroughly dissolved. Cool.

Basic bar measurements

Jigger	Usually 1 ounce
Teaspoon or bar spoon	⅛ ounce
Dash (as of simple syrup, orgeat, grenadine, lemon juice)	¼ ounce
Dash (as of bitters)	⅛ teaspoon
Scoop (of ice)	About 1 cup
Juice of 1 average lime	1 ounce
Juice of 1 average lemon	1½ ounces

ABOUT WINE

When I was growing up, I was always allowed a certain amount of wine with my meals, always with some water. We drank only red wine in my family then; and to this day, I like red wine mixed with water. It's just as good mixed as drunk straight. I was invited to a very fine fishing club recently; and an old friend brought along an exceptional bottle of French red wine. I proceeded to pour mine with half water, and my friend was shocked. But give me one good reason why I shouldn't mix my wine with water if that's the way I like to drink it! When I drink wine, I drink a lot of it, and I like big mouthfuls; I don't like to swish it around in my mouth. There are a lot of Frenchmen who drink good wine mixed with water. Just make this experiment: Sit with a friend and each of you drink a bottle of wine—one bottle straight and one mixed with water. One guy is not going to be nearly as *pompet* as the other guy. You don't drink to get drunk, you drink for enjoyment.

And that's the way I feel about wine: drink what *you* like when you like it and how you like it.

People were writing about wine long before the time of Christ, and people have drunk more wine than any other drink outside of beer and water. Yet, it surprises me that we know so little about wine. Now I'm not going to go into a big poo bah on wine; I'm only going to try to tell you a few truths about what I know on wine and what you should do to see that you get wine that's fit to drink.

Now, let's get the thing in perspective. France has fifty million Frenchmen, and devotes much of her land to growing grapes for wine. The U.S.A. has two hundred twenty-five million people and devotes only a small part of California and New York to seriously growing wine grapes, with the consequence that every winery here can sell its output the day it crushes its grapes.

So, if a California winery wants to make good wine, it does so for two reasons: First, it gets a better return profitwise. Second (and maybe this should be first), it gets some pride in doing a good job. So you have larger wineries with large capacities for making fine wines, and those with capacities for making ordinary wines of good quality—and some quite high quality. Then you have small wineries making absolutely superb wine and some making absolutely lousy wines.

How do you find good wines? You try to find a merchant who specializes in wine, especially California wines; these are hard to find. Drink wines and compare, look around, read what you can, then find the wines you want and buy them. Then the most important thing of all is to put your wine down in storage to put some age on it.

Most California wineries do not have the space, finances, or time to put the full age on their wines. Most of them sell their wines just as soon as they are mature enough to sell, say one or two years on the whites and three years on the reds and sooner. California wines should have more age than French wines to reach their goodness. Most California wines can stand at least two to five years of age to reach perfection. You can provide this in your own cellar, and you'll have pride and great satisfaction with your results.

Now, you can't make a silk purse out of a sow's ear; neither can you make poor wine into great wine by aging it. That goes for French as well as California wine. So take care in choosing the wine for setting up your cellar. There are many sincere people in the industry who will advise you. My thoughts here may help in some ways. For example:

Pinot Chardonnay comes from a small grape with a small bunch which grows only in certain areas. This makes the juice cost more than juice from other grapes. So some wineries do a lot of blending with Pinot Chardonnay to stretch it; and the full flavor goes out the window. You could age some of those Chardonnays for ten years and they would be nice but not great. But some of the purer ones can be grand.

Some of the whites such as Rieslings, Traminers, and Sylvaners will stand two to five years of age, but you shouldn't keep them longer than that. The whites such as Sauvignon Blanc, Semillon, Pinot Chardonnay, and Chenin Blanc can take a longer aging and develop their bouquet or nose in a little more time; they generally will hold longer.

Reds, such as Cabernet Sauvignon and Pinot Noir, now they're another thing. Buy enough so you can forget them for five or more years; drink something else in the meantime; they take a little time to develop. Get good ones when you buy them. (Actually, Pinot Noir will never be a great wine in this state. Go to your Cabernets.) Don't put down light reds for aging; you'd be wasting your time; in two to three years, they will have arrived; and they're what you can drink while you're waiting for your heavy reds to age.

Now I'll say a few words on the wines that I personally drink. Just for everyday drinking, I like Almaden Gewürztraminer or Wente Dry Semillon in the whites. In the reds: Louis Martini's Zinfandel or Mountain Barbera, or Charles Krug Zinfandel. For Sunday or company time: Stony Hill or Hanzell Chardonnay for white or Louis Martini or Beaulieu or Charles Krug Cabernet Sauvignon for red. Paul Masson has a good Cabernet and a good Emerald Dry Riesling. Almadén has a champagne. Now remember this: What I like doesn't mean that everything else is crap. There are a lot of small wineries that are good. I just happen to know the people who make the wines I've mentioned, and these wines please me. After all, I don't have to try to be nice to everybody in this book.

I've told you quite frankly that, to do a good job on wine, you've got to drink it by trial and error. If you think that you're going to become an expert in five easy years, you're crazy or exceptional. I know some men who have tried for twenty years, and they still don't know their *tochas* from a hot rock when it comes to wine.

Maybe you're wondering where I got my upbringing on wine. Well, it started when I was eight years old. After school, I filled wine bottles in my uncle's wine cellar right from the fifty-gallon casks. I was never allowed to drink the wine, only run my finger through the foam as it swirled from the hose coming out of the barrels into the funnel stuck in the bottle top.

So, of course, I've been associated with wine since I was born and I'm seventy, and in all that time, I have never been drunk on any kind of alcoholic beverage. Getting drunk is stupid. I've watched men do this to themselves to my sorrow and disgust.

Note: Each drink recipe yields one drink unless noted otherwise.

Trader Vic Daiquiri

When I started making mixed drinks, I took a trip to Cuba. Geez, it took one week by rail and boat to get to Havana. This was a thousand years ago.

When I finally got there, I found that there was only one place in the whole country where they made a daiquiri. That was the La Florida, and Constantino Rapalo presided over the bar. You walk in, and he's got a big pile of fresh limes in front of him. The joint could be full of people. He picks out a lime, cuts it, squeezes it into a regular milk-shake container, puts in a half ounce of maraschino, 2 ounces of rum, a teaspoon of bar sugar, and some shaved ice; he whirls it, and strains it through a strainer. Now this is *the* way to make a daiquiri.

Now, these days, if you do this at home with a high-powered drink mixer, you don't have to strain it, you can just pour it into a cold glass. But if you strain it, it will be even smoother, it comes out just like applesauce, and you can mound it up a little bit.

This is the real honest-to-goodness daiquiri, so help me Hannah!

1 lime
1 teaspoon bar sugar
¼ teaspoon frozen unsweetened
   Florida grapefruit juice
   concentrate, undiluted

½ ounce French Garnier
   maraschino
2 ounces light Puerto Rican rum

Finger-squeeze lime juice over a 12-ounce glassful of shaved ice in container of electric drink mixer. Add remaining ingredients. Blend well. Strain through medium-mesh kitchen strainer into chilled *tiki* stem champagne glass or other large saucer champagne glass.

Mai Tai

I've said this a million times. We originated this drink; we made the first Mai Tai; we named the drink. A lot of bastards all over the country have copied it and copyrighted it and claimed it for their own. I hope they get the pox. They're a bunch of lousy bastards for copying my drink.

Here is my original formula for the Mai Tai, as well as two contemporary formulas.

Mai Tai (Trader Vic's original formula)

2 ounces 17-year-old J. Wray and Nephew Jamaica rum
½ ounce French Garnier orgeat
½ ounce Holland deKuyper orange curaçao
¼ ounce rock candy syrup
Juice from 1 fresh lime
Fresh mint

Hand-shake all ingredients and then garnish with half of the lime shell inside the drink and float a sprig of fresh mint at the edge of the drink. The drink should be chilled nicely with a considerable amount of shaved ice in a large 15-ounce glass.

Mai Tai (a current formula)

1 lime
½ ounce orange curaçao
¼ ounce rock candy syrup
¼ ounce orgeat syrup
2 ounces Trader Vic Mai Tai rum or 1 ounce dark Jamaica rum and 1 ounce Martinique rum

Cut lime in half; squeeze juice over shaved ice in a mai tai (double old-fashioned) glass; save one spent shell. Add remaining ingredients and enough shaved ice to fill glass. Hand-shake. Decorate with spent lime shell, fresh mint, and a fruit stick.

Mai Tai (using commercial mix)

2 ounces Trader Vic Mai Tai mix
2 ounces Trader Vic Mai Tai rum
Fresh mint, fruit stick, and fresh lime (optional)

Fill mai tai (double old-fashioned) glass with shaved ice. Add mix and rum, and shake. Decorate with fresh mint and a fruit stick and fresh lime if you wish.

Margarita on the Rocks

I don't think that we Americans give tequila enough room. This is just one helluva nice liquor to make drinks out of. And a Margarita on the Rocks is an easy drink to make, it tastes nice, it's a beautiful drink.

Juice of ½ lime
½ ounce Triple Sec
1 ounce tequila

Shake in commercial electric drink mixer (or in shaker can with mixing glass) with ice cubes. Pour into an old-fashioned glass which has been rimmed with kosher salt.

Navy Grog

You can substitute three ounces of Trader Vic's Navy Grog and Punch rum for the three rums listed below.

3 ounces Trader Vic Navy Grog mix
1 ounce light Puerto Rican rum
1 ounce dark Jamaica rum

1 ounce 86-proof Demerara rum
Lime shell, rock candy stick, and fresh mint

Pour first four ingredients into mai tai (double old-fashioned) glass filled with shaved ice. Hand-shake. Decorate with a lime shell, rock candy stick, and fresh mint.

Suffering Bastard

Suffering Bastard got its name in Egypt. There was the Raffles Bar there in the Shepheard's Hotel in Cairo where they made a drink kinda like this one. There they called a bartender a bar steward. One fellow working there was pretty busy, and they started to call him the suffering bar steward, and soon it turned into suffering bastard.

This is my interpretation of that drink.

1 lime	**2 ounces St. James rhum**
½ ounce curaçao	**Lengthwise strip of cucumber**
¼ ounce orgeat syrup	**peel, cut 1 inch wide**
¼ ounce rock candy syrup	**Cucumber peel, lime shell,**
1 ounce light Puerto Rican rum	**fresh mint, and fruit stick**

Cut lime; squeeze juice into mai tai (double old-fashioned) glass filled with shaved ice; save one shell. Add curaçao, syrups, and rums. Hand-shake. Decorate with cucumber peel, spent lime shell, fresh mint, and fruit stick.

Maui Fizz

This is also called a Racquet Club Fizz.

½ slice pineapple	**2 teaspoons bar sugar**
1 egg	**1 ounce light Puerto Rican**
1 ounce lemon juice	**rum**

Blend all ingredients in an electric drink mixer with ½ scoop shaved ice. Pour into a footed iced tea glass.

Trader Vic Rum Fizz

1½ ounces light Puerto Rican	**1 egg**
rum	**½ ounce cream soda**
1 ounce lemon juice	**Grated orange peel**
2 teaspoons bar sugar	

Shake all ingredients except orange peel in commercial electric drink mixer (or in shaker can with mixing glass) with ice cubes. Strain into fizz glass. Sprinkle wth grated orange peel.

Banana Cow

I know guys who take tomato juice and Worcestershire sauce for a hangover and make themselves sick as hell. Now a hangover calls for a lot of therapeutic thought—something that's healing and soothing.

It used to be, in our early days, that when we opened up on Sunday morning, we had a half-dozen guys outside all lined up, waiting for a Banana Cow so that they could come to life. This is almost medicine, fellows. Try it.

1 dash Angostura bitters
1 whole banana
1 teaspoon bar sugar
1 dash vanilla

3 ounces fresh milk
1 ounce light Puerto Rican
    rum
½ scoop shaved ice

Blend in electric drink mixer. Serve in planter's punch glass or 12½-ounce tumbler.

Rum Cow

This is a morning drink too. It's especially good if you mix a little of any of the pungent rums with the Puerto Rican rum to make a fuller rum taste.

1 dash Angostura bitters
1 dash vanilla
1 teaspoon bar sugar

6 ounces fresh milk
1 ounce light Puerto Rican rum
Grated nutmeg

Shake first 5 ingredients in a commercial electric drink mixer (or in shaker can with mixing glass) with ice cubes. Strain into a planter's punch glass or 12½-ounce tumbler. Dust with grated nutmeg.

Hot Rum Cow

Sometimes you and your old lady come home and you're cold all the way through. A hot toddy doesn't do it. Nothing else does it. But if you make this and drink this—you can even drink it in bed—you'll get nice and toasty and you'll sleep like a log.

1 teaspoon bar sugar
1 dash Angostura bitters
1 dash vanilla
8 ounces very hot milk

1 to 1½ ounces light Puerto
    Rican rum
Grated nutmeg

Blend first 5 ingredients thoroughly in an electric drink mixer. Pour into a large heated mug or a planter's punch glass or tall tumbler. Dust with grated nutmeg.

Hot Buttered Rum

3 to 4 whole cloves
1 heaping teaspoon hot buttered
    rum batter (recipe below)
1½ ounces light Puerto Rican
    rum

Boiling water
Cinnamon stick

Preheat skull mug or other 6-ounce heatproof mug with boiling water. Put cloves and batter into mug. Add rum. Fill mug with hot water. Stir well. Hit with hot poker. Decorate with 8-inch cinnamon stick.

Hot Buttered Rum Batter

This is how you make hot buttered rum batter. Trader Vic Food Products puts out a batter made by the same formula, and you can buy it in a store and you don't have to make the batter yourself. But if you have to or want to make it yourself: this is the best way. Some recipes call for melting a gob of butter on top of the drink and all you get is a lot of greasy butter on your lips.

1 pound brown sugar	¼ to ½ teaspoon ground
¼ pound soft butter	cinnamon
¼ to ½ teaspoon ground	¼ to ½ teaspoon ground cloves
nutmeg	Pinch of salt

Beat sugar and butter together until thoroughly creamed and fluffy; beat in nutmeg, cinnamon, cloves, and salt.

Southern Comfort Mint Julep

Oh heck. This is something I first made up a long time ago. When Southern Comfort first came out, nobody was buying it. In fact, ours was the first bar in California to buy a lot of Southern Comfort. So we made up two or three drinks with it.

Now if you want to give yourself or your friends a nice little change, do this drink.

You can make a dozen of these and put 'em in the freezer and keep them all day until you're ready for 'em. You know, just crush that old mint and put in ice and mint and fill it up with Southern Comfort and jiggle it up a little bit and go stick it in the icebox or freezer for a half hour and that's the damnedest drink—if you like mint juleps. That's all there is to it—no sugar, just mint and ice and Southern Comfort.

Don't muddle the mint too much or you'll get the bitter taste as well as the pleasant.

Fresh mint sprigs
Southern Comfort
Powdered sugar

Clap mint sprigs between hands to loosen oils. In a 12-ounce glass, alternate layers of shaved ice and a total of 6 or 7 mint leaves to fill glass. Muddle thoroughly. Fill glass with Southern Comfort. Stir. Chill for 30 minutes to 1 hour before serving. Decorate with fresh mint leaves dusted with powdered sugar.

Champagne Apricot

Sometimes you make up a drink that is the absolute end. Well, this Champagne Apricot is the absolute end.

If you want to get a party started and you want a surprise, you just make this Champagne Apricot and you will have the damnedest party ever in your life. I guarantee it. If you don't believe me, try a couple for yourself first. This is really bordering on a love potion!

1 whole peeled canned apricot, frozen
¾ to 1 ounce Southern Comfort
Chilled champagne

Place frozen apricot in chilled saucer champagne glass; pour Southern Comfort over it. Add champagne to fill glass.

Note: To freeze apricots, drain apricots and place one in each cube compartment of ice-cube tray.

Drunken Apricot

Here is the same idea in larger portions. Freeze the apricots same as above. Don't knock all the bubbles out of the champagne when you mix it with the Southern Comfort.

1 fifth Southern Comfort
3 fifths chilled champagne
35 to 50 whole peeled canned apricots, frozen

Pour Southern Comfort over a large block of ice in a punch bowl. Let chill. At serving time, add champagne. Gently mix by turning ice around. To serve: put an apricot into a champagne glass, and fill the glass with the punch. Makes about 50 servings. But this is so damn good that I don't think you can count on 50, more like 35.

Southern Comfort Old-Fashioned

1½ ounces Southern Comfort   **1 dash Angostura bitters**
½ ounce water   **Lemon peel and cherry**

Pour first 3 ingredients into a 10-ounce old-fashioned glass filled with ice cubes. Stir well. Add a twist of lemon peel and a cherry.

Mai Tai Rum Old-Fashioned

If you like a good pungent rum that's got a good flavor, you'll find this a very nice drink. We blend this Mai Tai rum from five or six different rums from different islands.

1½ ounces Trader Vic Mai Tai rum	2 dashes maraschino cherry juice
½ ounce water	Lemon peel, fruit stick, and
2 dashes Peychaud bitters	fresh mint

Pour first 4 ingredients into a 10-ounce old-fashioned glass filled with ice cubes. Stir well. Add a twist of lemon peel. Decorate with a fruit stick and fresh mint.

Eastern Whisky Sour

Whisky sours—a-a-ach! But we made a drink we call an Eastern Sour. Really it's a small whisky punch. And it's a lot more fun to drink than a stinkin' old sour, acid whisky sour.

½ orange	2 ounces bourbon
½ lemon	Fresh mint sprig and fruit
1 dash orgeat syrup	stick
1 dash rock candy syrup	

Squeeze orange and lemon juice over ½ scoop shaved ice in a 16-ounce double old-fashioned glass; drop spent shells into glass. Add orgeat, rock candy syrup, and bourbon. Fill glass with shaved ice, and shake. Decorate with fresh mint sprig and fruit stick.

Scorpion Punch

I was once invited to a cocktail party in Honolulu, and as I walked into the garden, somebody handed me a coconut filled with a Scorpion. The coconut was my only glass for the evening and the punch bowl was a barrel. Believe me, the thing was lively —try it at your next party.

1½ fifths light Puerto Rican
  rum
2 ounces gin
2 ounces brandy
1 pint lemon juice
½ pint orange juice

½ pint orgeat syrup
1 tenth gallon dry white table
  wine
2 sprigs fresh mint
Gardenias

Mix well all ingredients except gardenias; pour over ice cubes in a punch bowl. Let stand for 2 hours. Add more ice. Garnish with gardenias. Serve in punch cups or coconut cups. Serves 12.

Trader Vic Rum Cup

1 orange
1 lemon
1 lime
1 ounce lemon juice

2 ounces orange juice
1 ounce orgeat syrup
1 ounce Siegert's Bouquet rum
3 ounces light Puerto Rican rum

Cut orange, lemon, and lime. Squeeze juice over 2 scoops shaved ice in container of electric drink mixer; save shells. Add remaining ingredients. Blend. Pour into large Trader Vic scorpion bowl or other large-bowled compote. Decorate with spent orange, lemon, and lime shells. Serves 2.

Tahitian Rum Punch

This is the formula for a real Tahitian rum punch—the way they do it at a party in a home in Tahiti.

I first made this when I was opening a restaurant in Honolulu. (This was before the War. I don't have a restaurant there any more. The guy stinks who runs one there now and uses my name.)

Anyway, one day when I was working on this opening, Carrie Guild came in. She's an old friend who lived in Tahiti for years and was then living in Honolulu. So I asked her, "Carrie, how do you make a good punch?" And she said, "Well, this is how I make it when I have a party at home."

It's a rigmarole, but it's one helluva recipe.

2 pounds brown sugar

5 dozen oranges

4 dozen lemons

3 grapefruit

10 bananas

2 mint sprigs

10 fifths dry white table wine

6 fifths light Puerto Rican rum

1 fifth dark Jamaica rum

Put sugar into a large crock. Squeeze juice from oranges, lemons, and grapefruit; add juices and all spent shells to crock. Slice in bananas. Add mint and wine. Let stand overnight. Next day, add the rums. Strain off and discard the fruit pulp and citrus shells. Stir punch well. Pour over a large block of ice in a punch bowl (or a barrel). Let mixture chill. Serve in punch cups or coconut cups. Serves about 100.

Trader Vic's Wine Cup

This is the formula for our wine cup. There're a million other formulas for these things. You can fudge this, you can do that, you can splash it on the wall.

If you're having sort of an outdoor thing—or an indoor thing—anyway a hot-day kind of thing, you'll find that a wine cup is an awfully nice nice way to quench your thirst.

You can use a wide variety of wines. We're just saying white wine in this one. You could use red wine or rosé wine. Now I wouldn't try a sherry or port; you might get an *ick* result. And the variety of fruits that you use gives you the variety of possible flavors; you can use a lot of different fruits or leave everything out and use just peaches. You can make it in a pitcher, a pot, or a five-gallon oil can. But you should have a lot on hand because you're going to drink a lot of it. It's good.

6 large strawberries, sliced

2 oranges, thinly sliced

2 lemons, thinly sliced

1 slice pineapple

1 large mint sprig

1 ounce Grand Marnier

1 ounce peach liqueur

1 ounce passion fruit nectar

1 fifth dry white table wine

Fill a 2-quart pitcher about 1½ inches deep with ice cubes. Insert part of the sliced strawberries, oranges, and lemons between ice and pitcher. Add another layer of ice cubes, repeating addition of sliced fruits. Repeat until pitcher is full of ice cubes and sliced fruits. Place pineapple slice on top; center with mint sprig. Pour Grand Marnier, peach liqueur, and passion fruit nectar over ice. Swizzle well with heavy swizzle stick until fruits are bruised. Add wine. Swizzle again until mixture is blended and chilled. Serve in white wine glasses. Serves 4 to 5.

Trader Vic food products mentioned in this book are available from:

Trader Vic's Food Products
Emeryville, California 94608

Index